JOSETTE MILGRAM

BEAUTY
FOOD
EAT WELL TO
LOOK BEAUTIFUL
BY
marie claire

beauty food

manger sain pour être belle

健康食べ、美しいがありなさい

mangiare sano per essere bella

съешьте здоровую и красивейше

comer sano para ser bonita

吃健康并且是美丽的

zu essen gesund, um schön zu sein

MURDOCH BOOKS

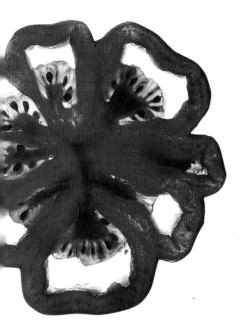

Contents

My looks need to be fed, too… with pleasure

MY HEALTH SOURCE

Pleasure: good for your health?

Eat to live—or rather, eat better to live better. Turn an obvious physiological truth into small (and big) pleasures on a daily basis and you may discover the most delicious way to prescribe your own medicine.

THE WORLD HEALTH ORGANISATION'S OFFICIAL DEFINITION OF HEALTH

'A state of complete physical, mental and social wellbeing.' Eating well is involved with all three. Our food is, after all, destined to become a part of us. Hence the need to pay attention to (and enjoy) what we put on our plates. Relaxing and treating ourselves to a delicious meal, without any second thoughts, is the best way to remind ourselves that our body is our best friend.

FOOD FOR THOUGHT

Food that tastes good should also—as a matter of good taste—perform well nutritionally. The perception of different textures, the development of the taste molecules, the prompting of the taste buds to do their work are all linked to receptors located in the oropharynx (back of the throat). They tell the brain what we are eating, and set off its taste memory. According to Laurence Salomon, chef and naturopath, the more pleasure we take in food, the more benefit we derive from what we eat. Depriving ourselves upsets the balance of our psychological relationship with food and drives us to the opposite extreme, overcompensating. The solution lies in pleasure. Thoughtful pleasure, where you really experience the food. If you adore chocolate, don't deny yourself… and you'll be safe from binges.

THE WORD FROM NUTRITIONIST DR ARNAUD COCAUL

author of *Le Plaisir Sans Les Kilos* (The Pleasure Without the Kilos; Marabout, 2008)

THE PLEASURE OF SINKING YOUR TEETH INTO LIFE… IT HAS BITE!

Chewing is supposed to increase your brain volume by stimulating circulation via the nerves located at the base of the teeth: the more you chew, the more oxygen is pumped into the brain.

THE MASTICATORY COEFFICIENT

This is an evaluation grid based on the number of 'paired' teeth: each tooth has a number and, without an opposing tooth (its 'antagonist'), it doesn't work any more. The molars (capable of grinding 100kg per square centimetre) and premolar teeth are essential to our nutritional health. Too often, we pay more attention to the aesthetic side of our smile.

Variety... to satiety

Some trends aren't far away from confusing food and religion: how about we lighten up a bit before sitting down to eat?

ORTHOREXIA

A real social illness, orthorexia is the ultimate form of food terrorism. Sufferers forbid themselves particular foods, which are demonised, and are preoccupied with eating the 'right' thing. Contradictory messages about food end up giving them a stomach tied up in knots! The nutritional cacophony is due to the fact that nutrition is a new science, still in the throes of evolution, and anyone can take advantage of it. You have to be very cautious about claims that are made. Statistically, the only reliable sources are cohort studies (randomly selected), which follow patients over ten years.

DOWN WITH THE TYRANNY OF NUMBERS: WE'RE ALL UNIQUE

It's not possible to fit us all into the same mould. The problem with RDIs (recommended daily intakes) is that they are based on averages. The majority of us don't live in countries where there are deficiencies of vitamins and trace elements. The problem with universal prevention campaigns is that their message gets sent to countries where it is not needed. Dietary supplements concern certain subsets of the population (the sick, immigrants, people suffering anorexia, the very old or future mothers who have specific needs). If you are not in one of these groups, **your body is perfectly able to get everything it needs from a balanced and varied diet**.

WHAT DO WE KNOW FOR SURE?

The benefits of fruits, vegetables and good fats, the need to limit salt and sugar, and **the joy of sitting down to enjoy a meal without feeling guilty** are all things to take on board.

THE WORD FROM NUTRITIONIST DR ARNAUD COCAUL
TOO MANY SUPPLEMENTS
We tend to over rely on supplements that disregard the complexity of our dietary needs and only provide extra amounts of an isolated element. Taken in excess, for example, vitamin C goes from being 'anti' to 'pro' oxidant—and ends up generating the free radicals it is supposed to fight. Frightening news items, like the killer pills that are supposed to make you thin, reinforce the fact that it's vital to seek out the advice of a doctor or pharmacist, and that it's dangerous to buy pseudo-medicines outside of the official channels, especially on the internet, with no quality control or guarantee.

Synchronise your watches to the right time

Our understanding of the human biological clock is getting better all the time. The same food won't always have the same effect (or ability to be absorbed), depending on the time of day it is eaten. Here's a 24-hour guide.

MORNINGS WITH MUSCLE

Bacon and eggs for breakfast? Sure. The proteins will boost dopamine levels and start your motor on the right track and **the lipids** will be greedily guzzled up by your enzymes. Remember: you're coming out of a quasi-fast, and simple sugars will prevent the elimination of fats stockpiled during the night.

A PROTEIN-RICH LUNCH AND A RESTFUL DINNER

For a stimulating lunch, bring on the proteins and fast sugars (the sugar-loving enzymes are up and running) to keep up concentration levels all afternoon. As the day goes on, our bodies tend to store more fat, so **bring on the carbohydrates in the evening** for a good night's sleep and stay away from fats, which help you to perform during the day, but will be hard to digest at night and will impact on a good night's sleep.

FINDING YOUR FOOD RHYTHM

The ideal day would contain three main meals and one or two lighter meals. But there are no hard and fast rules. If you're not hungry at breakfast time, it's not worth forcing the issue; you can balance things out over two or four meals. **Only young children can tell when they are truly feeling hungry;** it's our upbringing that herds us into meal times! Eating rhythms are cultural—we can eat dinner at 6pm in Canada or 11pm in Spain. And who knows how many meals our distant ancestors had in a day…

Snacking: your brain hates it

Unlike other parts of the body, the brain doesn't store energy reserves. The brain runs on glucose, with levels in the blood strictly monitored, and it doesn't appreciate fluctuations. The result? Sugary snacks upset your mood. When you start to eat it sets off a complex process: the more chaotic and frequent this is, the more the brain gets disoriented.

THE WORD FROM THE NUTRITIONIST

Thinking about a sweet snack in the afternoon? Biologically, it's the time your body needs it most and is best able to handle the sugar. And as for the famous 11am slump, it's not a myth: most traffic accidents happen around this time.

My basic needs now... and forever

It's all a matter of balance and variety: too much salt, too much sugar, too many bad fats and processed foods put our marvellous machine at risk... when all it wants to do is burn fuel efficiently! Nutritionist Dr Arnaud Cocaul explains.

EAT WELL, AGE WELL
The SU.VI.MAX study, conducted by Dr Serge Hercberg's team on 7000 volunteers, led to conclusions that feed into, most notably, the French National Health Nutrition Program (Programme National Nutrition Santé—PNNS). It shows, in particular, that women have better diets than men. The second study, SU.VI.MAX 2, is currently in progress.

EAT BETTER, LEARN BETTER
A diet high in essential fatty acids helps to keep the brain in good health and improves our learning ability. This has now been confirmed by the neurosciences: physical health has a direct influence on our mental abilities. This is one of the leads being followed up by the French Brain Research Federation in its fight against degenerative diseases.

THE SOLE PRIORITY: DIVERSITY

The more colourful a food is, the richer it is in antioxidants and vitamins. Colourful fruits and vegetables are high in fibre and need to be chewed; this way, the brain has time to be told what it's getting and the nutrients' potential is maximised.

GOOD FOR MY BRAIN AND MY MOOD

A well-oiled brain has a big appetite! It consumes 20 per cent of our oxygen and 40 per cent of our sugars. **It loves carbohydrates for mood and memory**, as well as **B vitamins**: B6 (salmon), B9 and B12 (liver, egg yolk). It gets its fix thanks to the **amino acids** in proteins, some of which are precursors to the neurotransmitters, which moderate our moods. Among these are **tyrosine**, which raises dopamine and noradrenaline levels, and **tryptophane**, which helps to synthesise serotonin. The brain also needs **polyunsaturated fatty acids** (the 'good' **omega-3s** from fish, canola oil and linseed), which contribute to a healthy hormonal balance and immune system, and let the brain get down to business. The brain will draw on its memory banks to use a particular glucose molecule, a particular hydrogen chain, fatty acids and proteins, like the dispatch centre of a central computer. Our **olfactory and sensory memory** centre is constantly improving. Over time, new flavours are added to it and we learn to appreciate new foods—not liking foods we don't know (food neophobia) is a self-protection mechanism. Nature can be dangerous, and a bad food choice can be fatal.

▶

▶ **GOOD FOR MY BONES**

Calcium is found in water, even tap water. Young girls should get extra calcium—because the physiological drop (the loss of muscle mass) begins at 20 and calcium helps protect against osteoporosis. Dairy products aren't the only solution: seaweeds such as wakame and the nori sheets in sushi contain six times as much calcium—reassuring if you are lactose-intolerant.

GOOD FOR MY MUSCLES

Eat proteins at each meal. If muscle mass isn't maintained, then your body doesn't burn as many calories. Muscle mass will burn energy (and keep your metabolism up), even when you're not exercising!

THE LITMUS TEST: ACID & ALKALINE

When we talk about acidity, it's not about foods that taste acidic: for example, fruits, even those that seem acidic, will have an alkaline pH level. As our system isn't equipped to deal with acidity, it will neutralise it by looking for bicarbonate within the body. An (animal-based) acidifying food can be compensated by two (plant-based) alkalinising foods. The basic guidelines are:

• **No meat without a vegetable**

• **No cheese without a fruit or salad** Fruit or salad is better than bread and cheese, a very acidic combination, which will accelerate bone demineralisation.

Magnesium

is involved in more than 300 biochemical reactions in the body. A lack of magnesium lowers our resistance to stress. It is found in green vegetables, some waters, whole grains and legumes and some nuts, with walnuts and hazelnuts at the top of the list. Vitamin B6 (grains, wheat germ, brewers' yeast, poultry) reinforces its effect.

Salt

Just 6g (or 1 teaspoon) a day (a pinch is equal to 1g) is ideal. More than this and the risk of cardiovascular disease increases. Salt is everywhere in mass-produced foods (deli meats, cheeses, bread, biscuits, soups and canned goods), and we use up 20–40 per cent of our daily intake when we add salt to water for cooking pasta.

THE WORD FROM THE NUTRITIONIST
Always taste before adding salt. Sweet or savoury, our sense of taste can be educated: our taste receptors, located at the base of the tongue, get used to finding flavour in less salty food. To help them along, increase the spices, herbs and other condiments.

The future on a plate

Hervé This, researcher with the French National Institute for Agricultural Research, pioneer of molecular gastronomy, scientific director of the Science and Food Culture Foundation, and partner of chef Pierre Gagnaire in his explorations at the cutting edge of culinary creativity, takes a look into the future of food.

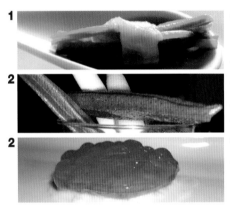

1

2

2

Hervé This talks about molecular gastronomy developed in collaboration with Pierre Gagnaire
"From artificial meat (green beans cooked al dente, hollowed out and filled with a foie gras mousse)[1] and the 'conglomelo' (a reinvented orange made with salmon roe)[2] it all starts from real ingredients. It's not about bankrupting the farmers. And when it comes to textures, we nurture contrasts. We are also working with the astronaut, Jean-Pierre Haigneré, on growing melon or carrot cells in space."

COOKING IS A CHEMICAL ART that isn't yet entirely rationalised. Our kitchen utensils haven't changed since the Middle Ages. We use a cooking method that is anything but sustainable: we waste 80 per cent of the energy we use, whether with gas or electricity. Animal rearing represents a terrible cost. And with the oil crisis, the concept of 'food miles' is becoming supremely important.

THE FUTURE

We can forget the scenarios that science-fiction used to predict, where a gelatinous mass would take on whatever taste and colour you want, or the 'nutritional pills' that Marcellin Berthelot threatened us with in 1900. He was forgetting that our system needs to regenerate and grow, and that it is full of water that needs to be replenished. We need to drink a lot, and water can't be compressed, so it can't be conveyed in tablet form! Everything has evolved from experience, and **we are far from having explored every avenue**.

THE DREAM would be to put together a set of extraordinary molecules, like the ones found in **the most common vegetables**, and make them into dishes that taste delicious and contain every one of the elements we need—while respecting the special qualities of their place of origin. But our tastes draw us to what we loved when we were small. **We are nourished first of all by love and culture**, then art and emotion, and finally by technique. All we can do is hope that, whether fashionable or not, the cooking of tomorrow takes this into account!

under my skin

2

MY BEAUTY SOURCE

The beauty of it all? Good food tastes sublime!

From the top of your head to the tips of your toes

A shiny crop of hair, nails as pearly as sea shells, smooth soft skin: it all comes from filling up your plate with vitamins.

DERMATOLOGIST DR DANIÈLE POMEY-REY'S PRESCRIPTION

VITAMINS B1, B2, B6 AND B5

These act on neurons and our skin is nothing more than nervous tissue: it should be cared for as such. It's one and the same tissue, the ectoblast, that turns into the ectoderm, becoming the nerves on the outside of the skin.

BEAUTIFUL MINERALS

Zinc (from red meat, shellfish and vegetables) helps to synthesise keratin, a basic skin material. **Iron** is important for the synthesis of all the metabolic reactions (the iron in red meat is easier to absorb than the iron in spinach, whatever Olive Oyl says!). **Magnesium** acts on the microcirculation and helps to nourish hair follicles and **selenium** is essential for the skin (found in fish, shellfish, oysters and turkey).

SOFT HAIR, STRONG NAILS

For shiny hair Include egg yolk, dark chocolate, nutritional yeast, watercress, orange-carrot juice in your diet.

To stop hair falling out Include oily fish, linseeds, red meat, oysters and wheat germ in your diet.

To strengthen weak, brittle nails Include whole grains, liver and egg in your diet.

Tip The antioxidants contained in grains and vegetables allow the plant to protect itself against free radicals and grow freely, and they have the same effect on our hair and nails.

CHAMPAGNE DINNER FOR TWO
• Oysters with cider vinegar and French shallots
• Braised veal with sage and carrots
• Fruit salad of orange, kiwifruit and pineapple

No moderation required
Sexual activity increases oestrogen levels, which makes skin soft and hair shiny.

Nutrition
and hydration for my skin

*The most mysterious organ,
our skin is a mirror of our emotions but also,
on a less poetic level, the quality of our diet.*

DERMATOLOGIST DR DANIÈLE POMEY-REY'S PRESCRIPTION

VITAMIN A: SMOOTH SKIN INSURANCE

It helps the skin renew itself: ideal if it's dry. Plant-based vitamin A, lycopene (found in **tomatoes**, also found in lower doses in **apricots, pink grapefruit, watermelon** and **guava**), provides support to the collagen fibres to ward off future slackening and preserve elasticity. Complement it with the animal-derived vitamin A, retinol (**egg yolk, raw butter**, **meat** and **offal**).

VITAMIN E: GET WRAPPED UP IN IT

The 'wrapping paper' vitamin, tocopherol (found in **hazelnuts** and **almonds**), works against the dehydration of what it envelops: the connective tissue around the muscles. It also slows down cell degradation in the same way as sun protection does.

VITAMIN C: IT'S GOOD FOR EVERYTHING

It's thanks to vitamin C that we produce cortisone, which acts on our mood and enables our adrenal hormones to function properly (it's these hormones that defend against stress, including the oxidative stress that ages us). Without our adrenal glands, life stops. In fact, there are stories about people who cured their illness with laughter (a natural serotonin-producing antidepressant) and vitamin C. Find it in **citrus fruits, red cabbage, kiwifruit, watermelon** and **strawberries**.

Be prepared before you expose yourself
An anti-UV prescription: you can help raise melatonin levels with the help of carotenoids: carrots, melon, apricot, kiwifruit, mango and all the exotic fruits, especially pomegranate.

BRUNCH FOR BEAUTIFUL SKIN
- Salad of smoked haddock and crab with grapefruit
- Scrambled eggs with stewed tomatoes
- Pancakes with bilberry (European blueberry) jam
- Mountain cheese
- Melon and watermelon with iced tea
- Smoothie of strawberries, kiwifruit and apricot

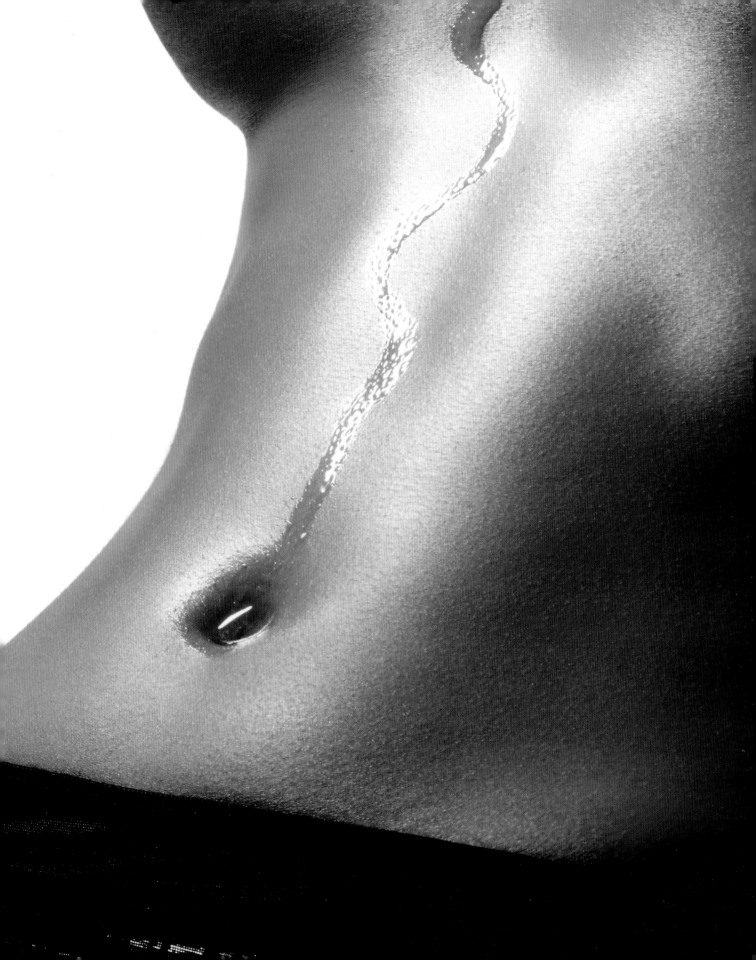

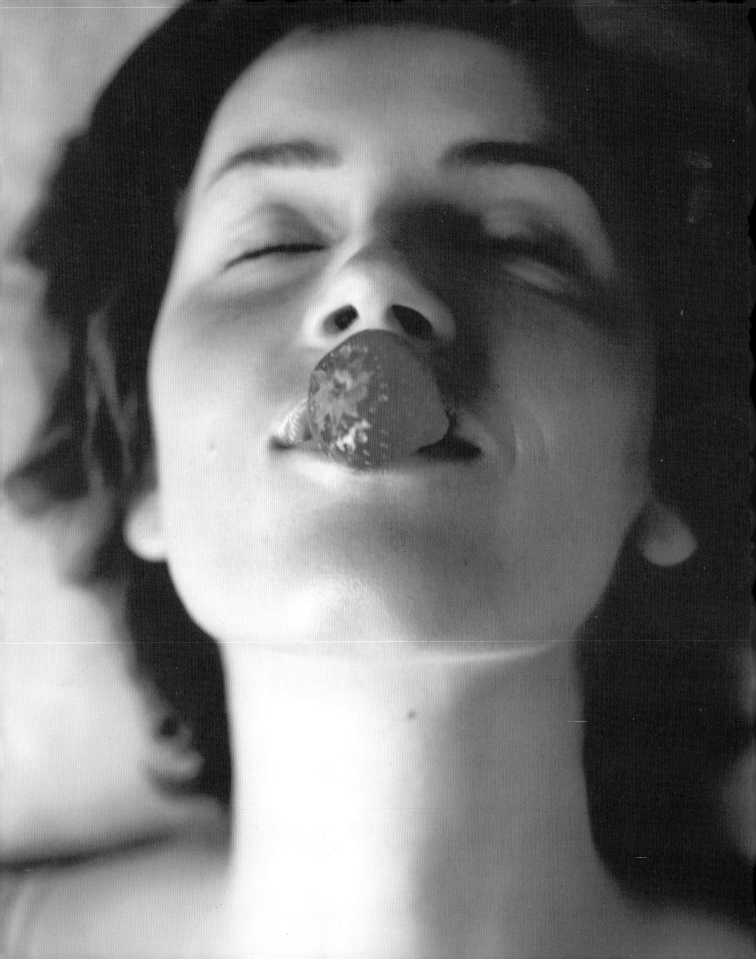

Beneath the surface:
purify and regularise

Our skin's glow is also about the regularity of our digestive system. A gentle clean-out guarantees a good result...

FIBRE: A GOOD MOVE(MENT)

The recommendation is to eat 25–30g of fibre a day. The average amount we consume in our Western diet is more like 15g a day.

Insoluble fibre Found in wheat bran. This kind of fibre speeds up the intestinal transit and increases the volume and frequency of bowel movements.

Soluble fibre Found in lentils, peas, beans, fruit and vegetables. This kind of fibre delays the emptying of the stomach, forms a gel in the intestine and slows down the absorption of glucose, cholesterol and triglycerides.

THE INTESTINAL FLORA IN FULL BLOOM

This fragile ecosystem of flora is indispensable for the proper absorption of nutrients. It can be upset by eating over-refined grains, taking certain medicines, too much stress... all of which can cause intestinal permeability ('leaky gut syndrome'), resulting in noxious molecules being absorbed into the system. Taking **probiotics** can improve certain skin problems, limit the adverse side-effects of antibiotics, and reinforce the immune system.

YOUR BEAUTY DINNER
- Rye bread with hummus
- Grilled salmon with gently stewed leeks
- Brown rice pilaf
- Lettuce with canola oil vinaigrette
- Apple compote with ground hazelnuts

THE WORD FROM THE NUTRITIONIST
A probiotic is a live microorganism that, when taken in sufficient quantity, offers benefits to the health of the host organism. These living germs feed on intestinal flora and improve the microbiota (microflora).

Real rehab in a week
Bring on the artichokes, whose chophytol helps drain the liver.

Menus for 20-somethings

Making the most of your youth, preparing for the future, and maintaining the rhythm of study, work and play… low-GI carbohydrates will give your brain a regular dose of glucose, and keep your spirits in the sunny zone.

Fresh or tinned, sardines can be adapted to suit all tastes.

BREAKFAST: CHOOSE FROM
- Green tea, 1 apple, plain yoghurt, rolled oats, raisins
- Coffee, a handful of almonds, wholemeal bread, a little butter, agave syrup
- Fresh orange juice, 2 eggs, sourdough bread, a few hazelnuts, lychee tea

MONDAY

LUNCH
- Sardines in olive oil
- Salad of green beans and potatoes
- Soy yoghurt with fresh fruit

DINNER
- Grilled pork chops
- Lentils with dijon mustard sauce
- Chocolate mousse with diced mango

TUESDAY

LUNCH
- Burghul tabouleh with tomatoes and prawns
- Granny smith apple

DINNER
- Herb and mushroom omelette
- Green salad
- Vanilla cream dessert

WEDNESDAY

LUNCH
- Shredded white cabbage and carrot salad with chicken and sesame seeds
- Wholegrain bread
- Grapefruit

DINNER
- Ham and prosciutto
- Wholemeal shell pasta with broccoli florets
- *Fromage blanc* with strawberry coulis

Chick peas: a concentrated kernel of energy, this is one versatile chick.

THURSDAY

LUNCH
- Spanish-style chickpea salad, with capsicum (pepper) and chorizo
- Caramelised pear

DINNER
- Grilled salmon fillet
- Cumin-spiced carrot purée
- Rice pudding with raisins

Omelette with mushrooms, dill and coriander (cilantro).

A perfect balancing act between tomato and feta, olive and canola oil (to combine the omegas).

FRIDAY

LUNCH

- Russian salad with tuna
- Lychees in syrup

DINNER

- Italian-style open sandwich: beef carpaccio, eggplant (aubergine), mozzarella cheese
- Curly endive salad with walnuts
- Apricots

SATURDAY

LUNCH

- Avocado with lemon
- Turkey curry
- Basmati rice
- Peach

DINNER

- Zucchini (courgette) spaghetti with Bolognese sauce
- Fontainebleau cheese

Chocolate mousse: the diced mango pairs perfectly.

SUNDAY

LUNCH

- Tomato and feta cheese with mint
- Mussels with french fries
- Blackcurrant sorbet

DINNER

- Hard-boiled eggs
- Creamed spinach
- Cinnamon-spiced apple compote

HEALTH TIPS
NO MORE HYPOGLYCAEMIA
Bring on super-concentration! Use wholegrains, *al dente* pasta, basmati rice and pulses in a menu that's familiar and easy to prepare.

Crème caramel: a delicious taste from childhood.

Menus for 35-plus years

Working hard at work and/or at home, cooking for yourself or for others, in the canteen, at work or on the run… not easy, but not impossible!

BREAKFAST: CHOOSE FROM
• Wholemeal bread, butter, green tea with mint, mixed fresh fruit
• Rolled oats, soy yoghurt or *fromage blanc*, walnuts or hazelnuts, apricots and raisins, orange juice, coffee

MONDAY

LUNCH
• Asian-style salad
• Coriander (cilantro) lamb kebab
• Celery purée with nutmeg
• Crème caramel

DINNER
• Seafood and green pea risotto
• Lamb's lettuce salad
• Pear

TUESDAY

LUNCH
• Red and white cabbage salad
• Pan-fried mackerel with cracked wheat
• Salad of oranges with currants

DINNER
• Tortilla omelette with potato and chorizo sausage
• Curly endive
• Fresh curd cheese with sweet chestnut purée

The dolls of the cabbage patch. Eat one of every colour.

WEDNESDAY

LUNCH
• Cucumber with balsamic vinegar
• Pork strips with green lentils
• Baked apple with redcurrant jelly

DINNER
• Cream of zucchini (courgette) soup
• Toasted sandwich of goat's cheese and walnuts
• Tapioca with almond milk

THURSDAY

LUNCH
• Palm hearts and tomatoes
• Turkey escalope with French shallots
• Quinoa with capsicum (pepper)
• Goat's cheese

DINNER
• Cream of white bean soup with savoury
• Belgian leek quiche
• Plain yoghurt with fresh fruit

Quinoa superstar.

A new take on the Sunday roast with a fragrant spice crust.

FRIDAY

LUNCH

- Tabouleh with mint
- Fillet of hake with *sauce verte*
- Steamed cauliflower
- Clementines

DINNER

- Salt cod and potato purée
- Green salad
- Sheep's milk cheese and quince paste

SATURDAY

LUNCH

- Shredded celeriac with canola oil mayonnaise
- Roast beef with two kinds of peppercorn
- Italian-style green beans
- Mixed fresh fruit salad with cinnamon

DINNER

- Green vegetable soup
- Chickpea patties
- Mesclun salad
- Peach emulsion with ginger

SUNDAY

LUNCH

- Prawn and avocado salad
- Rabbit with tarragon
- Purple rice
- Plum clafoutis

DINNER

- Homemade four-season pizza
- Lettuce
- Apple and blackcurrant compote

HEALTH TIPS

TOP OF THE MORNING

For breakfast, choose wholemeal bread or rolled oats which will keep you going the whole morning. Avoid the processed cereals aimed at children, especially when it comes to *their* breakfast. The manufacturing process makes these products behave in your system as if they were predigested: with the added sugar to improve the taste, you're guaranteed a mid-morning blood-sugar crash.

SIMPLIFY YOUR LIFE

Cook enough for two meals and freeze half for when you don't have time or energy.

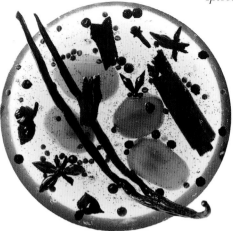

An exotic dessert: a gratin of fruit spiced up with vanilla and cinnamon.

Menus for
50-somethings

The biological clock doesn't stop. And neither do we. Are the lower hormone levels making your metabolism slower and causing you to put on weight? The dietitian's tip: move more and eat better!

MONDAY

LUNCH

• Leeks with vinaigrette

• Beef with olives

• Gently steamed broccoli

• Coconut cream dessert

DINNER

• White bean soup with savoury

• Tofu, radish and bean sprout salad

• Pineapple carpaccio

TUESDAY

LUNCH

• Quinoa-based tabouleh with raisins

• Herb-crusted tuna

• Runner (flat) beans

• Roquefort cheese

DINNER

• Baby vegetable and cashew risotto

• Prune and apple timbale

BREAKFAST: CHOOSE FROM

• Wholemeal bread, butter, berry tea, fresh fruit, acacia honey

• Rolled oats, soy yoghurt, hazelnuts and raisins, orange juice, green tea

Stuffed cabbage: full of vitamin C, it's the perfect balanced meal.

Chervil soup warms the cockles of the heart with its dollop of cream and scattering of parsley.

THURSDAY

LUNCH
- Mini spring roll
- Veal escalope with paprika
- Steamed fennel
- Banana baked *en papillote*

DINNER
- Braised stuffed cabbage
- Semolina pudding with soy milk and berries

Herring is a precious source of omega-3.

SATURDAY

LUNCH
- Baby vegetables *à la Grecque*
- Chicken with almonds
- Wild rice

DINNER
- Jamón or prosciutto
- Spinach with hazelnut oil
- Cinnamon-spiced pear compote

SUNDAY

LUNCH
- Tapenade
- Fish *pot au feu*
- Poached meringue with crème anglaise

DINNER
- Bruschetta with eggplant (aubergine) and fresh basil
- Curly endive salad
- Gratin of fresh fruit

Freshly sprouted bean shoots, full of vitality.

WEDNESDAY

LUNCH
- Hummus on toasted sourdough with linseeds
- Caribbean-style pork stew
- Sautéed celery and carrot
- Kiwifruit

DINNER
- Chervil soup
- Marinated herring with spices
- Steamed potatoes
- Orange

HEALTH TIPS

PHYTOESTROGENS These plant hormones have a similar effect to oestrogen. Soy is high in isoflavones; vegetables and whole grains in lignans, alfalfa and certain cabbages in coumestan.

VEGIES The cruciferous vegetables (cabbage, broccoli, cauliflower, kohlrabi) are said to protect us from certain cancers. They are an excellent source of vitamin C.

A MUST Cut out the snacking and sweets and avoid salt, which makes you retain water and dilutes calcium.

HERBAL TIP For the unpleasant side-effects of menopause: sage, evening primrose oil, alfalfa, hops.

FRIDAY

LUNCH
- Salmon tartare with three citrus fruits
- Red lentils with sesame oil
- Apple tart

DINNER
- Sweet potato soup
- Soft boiled eggs with salmon roe and cucumber ratatouille
- Curly endive
- Lemon mousse

3 my shape

MY BALANCE SHEET

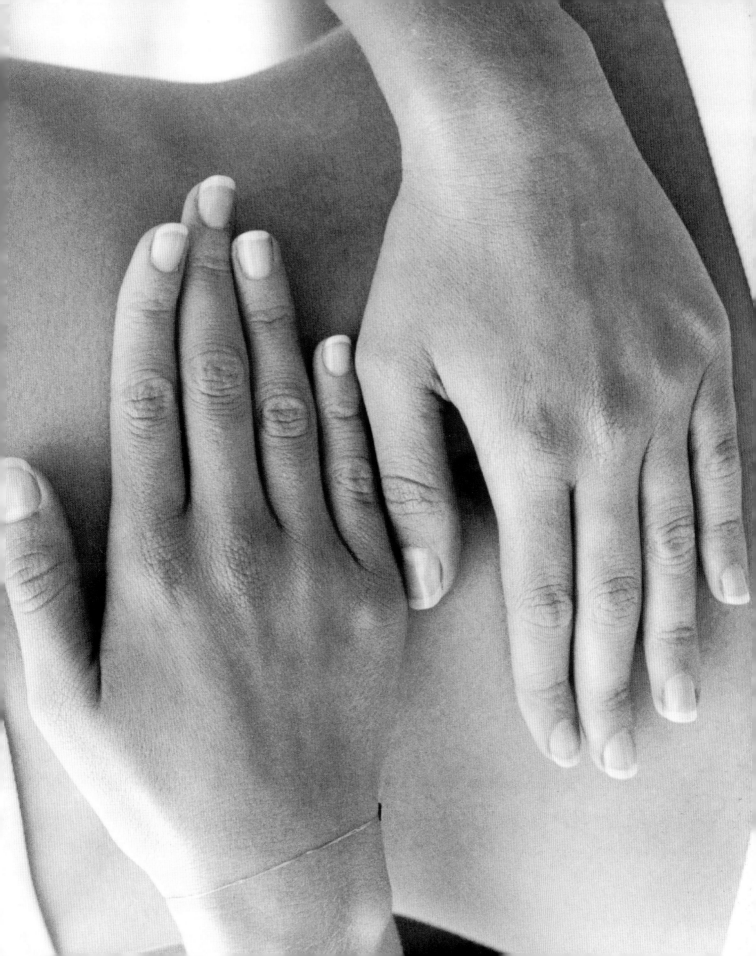

Dieting:
overthrowing the dictatorship

According to nutritionist Dr Xavier de la Cochetière, feeling good in your own skin means reclaiming your body's sources of 'food comfort'. So, down with the norm and embrace your form!

THE ANTI-FAT GRAIL

The impossible quest for the 'perfect' body is the result of media saturation: we're constantly fed diet information and dominant images of extreme thinness. Over the past 30 or so years, **the number of diets reported by the media has multiplied by 20.** At the same time, the number of individuals who are overweight has doubled. So, the more we talk about weight, the less we're able to control it. It's a vicious cycle with 'averages' and ideals thrust upon us, most of the time without the least scientific basis. Worse still, it works to wreck the image of food as natural, beneficial, essential and peaceful. **Research has found 73 per cent of women of 'normal' weight aren't happy with their bodies and 98 per cent of us want to be thinner!** Fortunately, over the past few years, there has been some lessening in the pressure to conform to a norm. Voices advocating free choice and pleasure are starting to be heard.

THE WORD FROM THE NUTRITIONIST

Excess weight is, above all, due to the loss of 'regulatory' behaviours that our body has forgotten, behaviours that may have served as a defence when faced with the risk of overeating. It is essential to reacquaint ourselves with the habit of calmly giving the body everything it demands, and all the food comfort it needs. It is surprising to realise that, on a day-to-day basis, we attach so little importance to an act that is essential to our health and happiness.

The *right* weight … for me?

*Our physiological weight, our wellbeing weight…
Nutritionist Dr Xavier de la Cochetière offers some weighty
arguments to help shift our obsession with the scales.*

Calculating BMI

This is our weight divided by our height squared (or get a ready-made answer by having it automatically calculated on the internet).

- 18.5 or lower: underweight
- 24.9 or lower: normal
- 25–29.9: overweight
- 30 and over: obese.

For example, a young woman who is 1.65m tall will weigh (on average) between 50 and 65kg and would be obese above 80kg. But remember, these are guides only.

Waist circumference

For a woman, a waist measurement of more than 80cm indicates a higher risk of cardiovascular illness, diabetes and hypertension.

Current weight calculations are based on the **BMI** or **body mass index**: it has replaced the absurd equations that offer just one unique 'ideal weight'. The BMI allows for a more flexible interpretation, offering brackets of up to 10–12kg. Even more interesting is **bioelectrical impedance analysis** which, by measuring body fat, is able to detect people who may appear thin but have low muscle mass (often due to lots of dieting), and people who may appear overweight but have high muscle mass. These terms, however, still seem too dictatorial and, above all, highly impersonal. They only represent averages!

Much more coherent is the idea of our **physiological weight**, which is as specific to each of us as the colour of our eyes. But how do we know what ours is? Nothing could be simpler: if your weight **remains stable without any special effort** on your part to maintain it, then you don't have a weight problem. For those who are familiar with the torment of excess weight, rediscovering this physiological weight occurs when they reaccommodate the 'natural' signals (hunger, satisfaction, fullness) of the body. Our body is always doing everything it can to help us keep it stable… while we often spend our time ignoring its help and doing the opposite of what it suggests.

Eat less or eat better?

What if a few simple tips altered everything, without having to adjust our habits too much or completely change our tastes?

TAKE YOUR TIME AND SAVOUR YOUR FOOD (SIT DOWN)

The body has inbuilt **regulatory mechanisms**—as long as it is given the chance to take charge. Sitting down to eat, taking one's time and interrupting the stressful rhythm of the day enables us to absorb food better. A calmer afternoon and a more restorative night's sleep will then be on the cards as well.

LOWER THE DENSITY, RAISE THE VOLUME

This means increasing the amount on your plate by choosing foods with a high water content that fill you up: soup and high-fibre fresh fruits and vegetables. Chew well, for a good period of time, and, if you need to, vigorously (it's calming).

A tip for eating less: buy smaller plates to fool your fear of being deprived: you can pile them up high and it's psychologically reassuring!

LET YOUR TEETH DO THE WORK

Take the time to chew well instead of swallowing things whole: it's essential for good digestion. Our tiny grinders enable the enzymes in saliva to 'predigest' carbohydrates and, by the same token, eliminate rather than stockpile them—thus helping you lose weight without even thinking about it.

MAKE THE RIGHT CONDIMENT CHOICES

• cream (an emulsion of fat and water) rather than butter (100 per cent fat) • vegetable coulis • soy sauce • light and frothy mayonnaise, made with less oil and a stiffly beaten eggwhite or plain yoghurt

THE WORD FROM THE NUTRITIONIST

Dr Xavier de la Cochetière, in his book *Jetez Votre Balance, Vous Êtes Guéri(e)* (*Throw Away Your Scales, You're Cured;* Robert Laffont, 2008), advocates the idea of a wellbeing weight: a synthesis of physical, aesthetic and, therefore, psychological wellbeing. He first looks at changing the factors that contribute to excess weight: an overgenerous or unbalanced diet, disruptive food habits, a sedentary lifestyle, but also our stress management. He also looks at restoring a more relaxed relationship with food, experienced as a source of comfort and pleasure. These changes allow you to rediscover the joy of food and stabilise your weight, by eating better and sometimes even feeling that you're eating more than before.

The satisfaction ratio: taming your appetite

One of the secrets to controlling your weight? Being able to perceive your real needs: train yourself to recognise your satisfaction threshold, so you don't go past it.

One laboratory-tested possibility in response to the obesity problem: blocking the production of the hormone **ghrelin**, which is responsible for the sensation of hunger (its levels rise before meals and lower afterwards). For the moment, it seems to work… on pigs!

THE WORD FROM THE DIETITIAN

Not getting enough sleep may encourage excess weight and obesity. A 2007 study shows that those who get less than 7 hours of sleep a night have three times the risk of obesity then those who get 8 or 9 hours. Lack of sleep boosts levels of ghrelin (see above) and reduces leptin (the satisfaction hormone). Eating enough in the evening is important for a good night's sleep.

OTHER TIPS

Yes to walking (at least three hours a week). No to television (especially if you eat in front of it). No to snacking (instead, have five well-thought-out meals throughout the day).

BON APPETIT!

When you don't feel any hunger, you don't feel the pleasure of appeasing it. Recognising this is the key to relishing food.

THE 20 MINUTE RULE

Eating (more) slowly is the only way of giving the brain enough time to process the message: the sensation of fullness only arrives 20 minutes after the beginning of a meal! You realise this all by yourself when you **give yourself time** to savour your food.

SOOTHING THE APPETITE SOONER

Eat fruit and vegetables **in pieces** rather than as purées or compotes. Eat **hot dishes**: the stomach gently dilates and immediately launches the digestion process. And you don't eat as quickly. The trick: begin a cold meal, such as salad or sushi, with a bowl of soup or wash it down with tea.

NATURAL APPETITE SUPPRESSANTS

Psyllium It swells up and produces a feeling of fullness.

Konjac A powder that absorbs 100 times its weight in water.

At the opposite end of the spectrum, sugary foods with a very high glycemic index stimulate the appetite and encourage you to eat more than the body needs. The body adapts by stockpiling the excess in the form of fat.

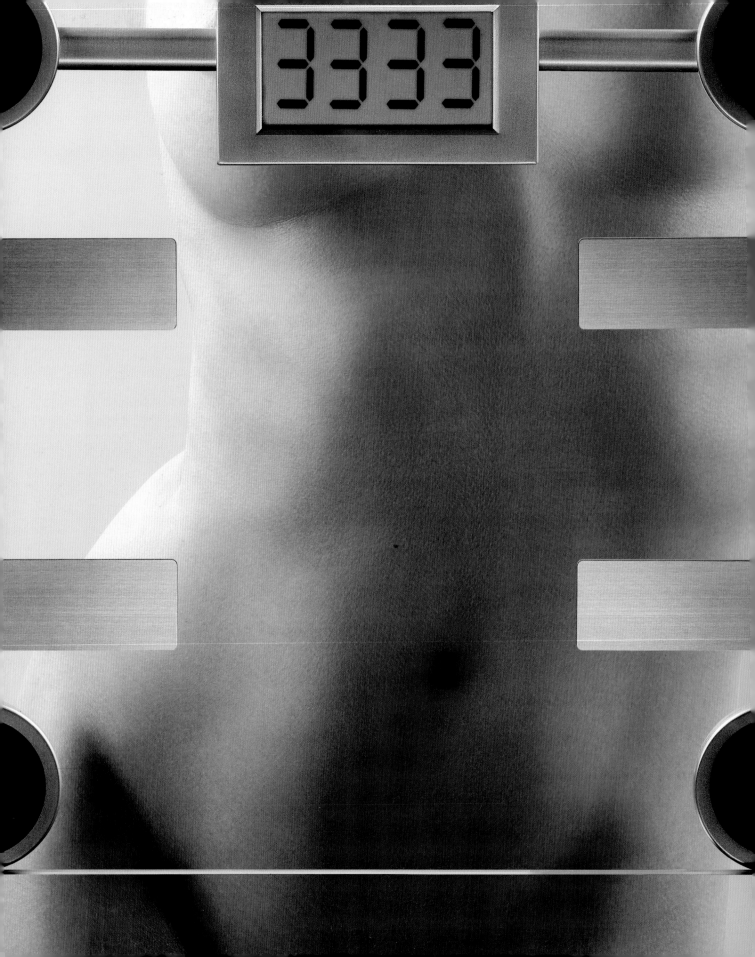

Strategies to beat the bloat

There's nothing more feminine than a soft rounded belly, but a swollen abdomen can be the first sign of poor digestion or a drop in hormone production.

A FLAT STOMACH: DIY

The first rule is to **eat slowly**. Not chewing properly prevents us from metabolising food. The result? Stockpiling, especially around the waist. Make sure to do a **targeted physical activity each day. Aim for good emotional management**. This is because stress bloats!

Stimulate your digestion Sip a cup of verbena tea.

Facilitate the intestinal transit Probiotics are just the thing.

AVOID

• Mustard, which inflames the mucous membranes.

• Soft drinks, even 'light' ones.

• Chewing gum, even sugar-free.

AFTER MENOPAUSE

The **glycaemic index diet** consists of avoiding certain foods (beer, doughnuts, white rice, potatoes) and instead choosing foods that are high in fibre with a low glycemic index (brown rice, wholemeal bread, green beans, oranges and yoghurt).

Bloated with water?
In fact, our body is only made up of about 60 per cent water (compared to 65 per cent in men), but this level can drop to as little as 30 per cent of overall weight in cases of obesity. When people talk about water retention, they're actually talking about retaining salt! Which explains why certain forms of oedema (water retention) can be treated, paradoxically, by drinking lots of water as this eliminates the excess salt.

HERBAL TIPS
Draining herbs: meadowsweet, artichoke, blackcurrant, orthosiphon.
Taming the appetite: guarana, caralluma and St John's wort (for sugar cravings).
Weight loss aids: sweet clover, orthosiphon, guarana.
Red vine leaf: these autumn leaves are high in tannins and anthocyanins, which strengthen the veins and so lighten the legs.
Galangal: encourages the elimination of fats and increases libido.

Sports support: move to get ahead

A sedentary lifestyle is our number one enemy. It's responsible for excess weight and sluggish digestion, among other ills. On the other hand, a well-chosen physical activity doesn't necessarily require you to be a sports nut, according to nutritionist Dr Arnaud Cocaul.

Central heating: the enemy within
The fact that our body no longer has to defend itself against temperature fluctuations partly explains our generation's problem with excess weight.

Muscle burns fat
It's magic: the more muscles you develop, the more calories you use—even when you've stopped moving. It also cheers you up, because sport is an anti-depressant.

Getting fit at my desk
Posture stools with springs, which keep you in perpetual movement to maintain your position, increase your energy output.

THE WORD FROM THE EXPERT
According to one study, physical activity stimulates the secretion of a protein, BDNF (brain-derived neurotrophic factor), which diminishes appetite.

SEDENTARY? OUT THE DOOR!
Being physically active doesn't have to mean signing up to a gym: we tend to confuse physical activity with training. The trick? Work out how active you are by calculating the daily number of steps you take with a **pedometer.** If all goes well, 5000 to 10,000 steps per day (or the equivalent of 3–6km) are more than enough. This type of exercise is also worth more than isolated bursts of strenuous effort with nothing in between, like the 'weekend jogger'. **And even if sport alone doesn't make you lose weight**, it does help reduce the spare tyre—and helps you to get more in touch with your body.

Find balance Swimming is good, but the 200 calories used up during a 1.5km swim will be wasted if you then eat a 500-calorie steak and chips. And remember that you can't put too much faith in the gym counters that say you've used up 2000 calories!

How to get the 30 minutes of physical activity recommended per day? This is equal to 30–45 minutes gardening; 8km bicycle ride; a 20-minute swim; running for 15 minutes; or climbing stairs for 15 minutes.

SCIENCE NOTE
A **calorie** is a unit of calorific energy representing the amount of heat required to raise the temperature of a gram of water (from 14.5°C to 15.5°C).

No more ready-made diets!

They come around with seasonal regularity and have kept us yo-yoing for generations. What if we could melt away old ideas as easily as kilos? But this is not easy (at least, not for all).

ONE-SIZE-FITS-ALL DIETS: THE WORD FROM DR ARNAUD COCAUL

Prevention can't be universal, including against obesity. We need to be educated about food, rather than about nutrients, apart from cases where there are risk factors for specific population groups. Scientific studies back this up: in opposition to food extremism, it's important to be able to take a critical step back and **stop thinking of extra weight as an illness.** Studies published in October 2007 in the *Journal of the American Medical Association* and the *New England Journal of Medicine* found that overweight individuals had greater longevity than others. So clearly we shouldn't force everyone to lose weight!

THE WORD FROM DIETITIAN PATRICIA DUROU

What diets have in common is that they're all more or less questionable, and they all 'work' for a time if properly followed. Regaining weight is often inevitable, via a boomerang effect that returns us to our former eating habits. Adjust habits gently and over the long term, taking psychological factors into account and incorporating physical activity, to get out of the vicious circle of **deprivation/frustration/compulsion** that is only encouraged by an overly strict and monotonous diet. Avoid situations of temptation with alternatives (having a bath, going out, calling a friend). A bit difficult to put into practice in the beginning, but if you persevere, it's self-satisfaction guaranteed.

Over the following pages are examples of specially designed slimming (but not starvation) menus according to your activity level and temperament.

A brief history of dieting
- Horace Fletcher chewed each mouthful 32 times (once for each tooth) versus 60 times for Georges Ohsawa (the founder of macrobiotics).
- Guelpa (1911): fasting and enemas.
- Dr Leven (1920): 10 days of herbal teas and milk.
- Hypocaloric diets (Gesta, Mayo Clinic): you count everything!
- Low-carbohydrate diets (Atkins): you eat less sugar to melt fats.
- Food-combining diets: pioneered by Dr Hay (1927).
- Not to mention the soap diet (yum!), gastric banding or barbaric jaw-wiring.

To substitute or not to substitute?
Protein powder sachets, invented in 1962, are an easy option, since you simply skip a meal. But this imbalanced 'diet' leads to problematic food habits. You're better off adopting good everyday habits and preparing truly pleasurable meals.

Summer menus for super-energy

Easy-to-prepare meals, designed to keep you satisfied, even when you're overcommitted. These always include a raw vegetable (dressed with good oil) and a raw fruit for the vitamins.

BREAKFAST: CHOOSE FROM

- *Fromage blanc* (20 per cent fat), 1 punnet raspberries, 2 slices buttered bread, lemon tea
- Plain yoghurt, 3 tablespoons of unsweetened cereal, hazelnuts, a slice of melon, coffee

MONDAY

LUNCH

- Cucumber with mint
- Whiting with garlic cream and tomato *concassée* (peeled, seeded and finely diced tomato)
- Brown rice
- Apricots

DINNER

- Herb-stuffed eggplant (aubergine)
- Lettuce
- Light tiramisù with *fromage blanc* and fruit

TUESDAY

LUNCH

- Melon
- Grilled beef with lemongrass
- Russian salad of spring vegetables
- Plain yoghurt with blackberries

DINNER

- Burghul tabouleh with mint and smoked salmon
- Summer fruit kebab

WEDNESDAY

LUNCH

- Crudités dressed with canola oil and accompanied by *kasha* (toasted buckwheat)
- Grilled prawns with green peppercorn
- Ashed goat's cheese

DINNER

- Wheat salad with baby spinach and chicken breast
- Vanilla-poached peach

Fresh pasta with clams and baby vegetables: make a meal of it.

THURSDAY

LUNCH

- Fennel and endive with lemon
- Steamed halibut fillets
- Ratatouille
- Strawberries with mint

DINNER

- Gazpacho
- Soufflé omelette with cheese
- Nectarines

Fun and exotic, fruit kebabs with a sweet coulis.

Prawns on the barbie: don't eat the shells to avoid the carcinogenic charcoal. But even when barbecued without their shells, the carcinogenic particles are only a problem in high doses, and fruit and vegetable fibre will minimise the time it spends in the intestine.

HEALTH TIPS
FRUIT AND VEG: IT'S THE DOSE THAT MATTERS

Steamed vegetables, as many as you like, in big, beautiful mixed salads, which are as enjoyable to make as to eat. The most sugary **fruits** are cherries and grapes, so don't overindulge in them, especially between meals. Summer is the season of grilling food **on the barbecue**, or, even better, on the hot plate (the fat doesn't drip into the fire), enhanced with delicious marinades: flavoured oils, lemon, herbs, soy sauce, garlic, Tabasco, chilli, honey, wine, vinegar.

FRIDAY
LUNCH
• Radishes and broad (fava) beans served *à la croque au sel* (raw with salt on the side)
• Lime-marinated monkfish kebabs
• Zucchini (courgette) with basil
• *Fromage frais* with herbs
DINNER
• Tagine of chicken breast with sweet potato
• Rocket (arugula) salad with smoked duck breast
• Mirabelle (yellow) plums

SATURDAY
LUNCH
• Tomato with mozzarella cheese
• Veal strips
• Baby carrots with fresh thyme
• Nectarine
DINNER
• Pasta with baby vegetables and clams
• Curly endive
• Cherry soup

SUNDAY
LUNCH
• Asparagus with chives
• Scallops with baby potatoes
• Watermelon granita
DINNER
• Green, yellow and white bean salad with French shallot vinegar
• Ham
• Crema Catalana

Broad (fava) beans were the original ingredients of cassoulet.

Winter menus
for super-energy

Want to increase the micronutrient density of your diet? No empty calories, but vitamins and mineral salts that are vital for physical and mental wellbeing, plus nuts, whole grains, pulses and good oils.

BREAKFAST: CHOOSE FROM
- Mineral-rich: 2 slices of bran bread, almond butter, 1 kiwifruit, oolong tea
- Vitamin-rich: 1 slice of ham, dried figs, 1 orange, coffee

MONDAY

LUNCH
- Grated carrot with poppyseeds
- Sautéed lamb with prunes
- Penne pasta
- Poached apple with cinnamon

DINNER
- Mixed vegetable soup with red kidney beans and broad (fava) beans
- *Fromage blanc* with bilberry (European blueberry) purée

TUESDAY

LUNCH
- Chicory (witlof) with walnuts and mandarins
- Lemon chicken
- Red lentils
- Pineapple mousse

DINNER
- Salmon *en papillote* with julienned vegetables
- Light lemon pumpkin pie

WEDNESDAY

LUNCH
- Artichoke hearts
- Grilled turkey escalope
- Broccoli with ginger
- Pear compote

DINNER
- Chickpea casserole with paprika and diced ham
- Yoghurt with dried apricots

Chicory (witlof): it has a very seductive bitterness.

Guinea fowl and cabbage: a very healthy combination that's perfect energy food.

THURSDAY

LUNCH
- Celery vinaigrette
- Monkfish curry with basmati rice
- Roquefort cheese

DINNER
- Chestnut soup
- Hard-boiled eggs with creamed spinach
- Orange fruit salad

Lemon pumpkin pie: a crust with just a little sugar that marries sweetness and lightness.

SUNDAY

LUNCH

- Oysters with tuna tartare
- Guinea fowl with cabbage
- Dark chocolate cream dessert

DINNER

- Red rice pilaf with prawns
- Sultana grapes

HEALTH TIPS

CARBS: IT'S THE DOSE THAT MATTERS

The rule: **just one starch per meal**, chosen from the low-GI range of foods (wholemeal pasta, basmati rice, pulses). Aim for 150–300g cooked weight, depending on your amount of physical activity.
So save bread (wholemeal or wholegrain) for meals with no starch and limit it to 2 pieces.

FOR A MORE ACTIVE BODY AND MIND

Increase vitamin B and C, iron, magnesium and zinc, the key nutrient for the immune system.

FRIDAY

LUNCH

- Beetroot with alfalfa sprouts
- Hake cooked *en papillote*
- Gently stewed leek and carrot
- Cantal cheese

DINNER

- Rice vermicelli noodles stir-fried with pork and mushrooms
- Mixed winter fruit salad

SATURDAY

LUNCH

- Broth with tapioca
- *Pot au feu* of lean beef, vegetables and tomato sauce
- Custard cream

DINNER

- Creamy split pea soup
- Stir-fried tofu with hazelnuts
- Shredded Chinese cabbage
- Kiwifruit

Oysters and tuna: an irresistible cocktail of iodine (100g oysters provides 90 per cent of our daily needs).

Summer menus:
zen version

Not a short-term revolution (so tiring and unreliable), just long-term evolution! Four goals: to eat better, to give yourself pleasure, to feel good… and to lose weight. Strive for calm and pleasure: stress leads to snacking and bingeing and, on top of it all, you lose weight more slowly.

Asparagus: 92 per cent water and very high in fibre, it contains calcium, magnesium, iron and vitamins A, B, C and E. Steaming preserves its nutrients and delicate taste.

BREAKFAST: CHOOSE FROM
• Traditional: toasted sourdough bread, a little butter, fruit compote with no added sugar, jasmine tea
• Almonds and hazelnuts, a bowl of fruit salad, soy yoghurt, lemon infusion

Exquisite lime-marinated bream.

MONDAY

LUNCH

• Rice salad with crab, red radish and green capsicum (pepper)
• Strawberries puréed with almond cream

DINNER

• Cucumber soup
• Steamed green peas with diced smoked ham
• Yellow nectarines

Freshly rinsed nectarines.

TUESDAY

LUNCH

• Baby leaf garden salad
• Bream ceviche
• Celeriac purée
• Soy yoghurt with bilberries (European blueberries)

DINNER

• Light savoury clafoutis with Mediterranean vegetables
• Lettuce
• Candied melon with honey

WEDNESDAY

LUNCH

• Grated carrot and apple salad
• Basmati rice with seafood
• Peaches

DINNER

• Round zucchini (courgettes) stuffed with goat's cheese
• Stewed rhubarb

FRIDAY

LUNCH

- Fennel carpaccio with coriander (cilantro)
- Pesto-marinated beef kebabs
- Green beans
- Comté cheese

DINNER

- Purple potato, tuna, hard-boiled egg and black olive salad
- Summer fruit

SATURDAY

LUNCH

- Spanish melon
- Chicken Basquaise
- Lemon sorbet

DINNER

- Gazpacho of watermelon with parsley
- Buckwheat crepe filled with caramelised onions
- Apricots

SUNDAY

LUNCH

- Green asparagus
- Grilled sea bass
- Eggplant (aubergine) with olive oil
- Light berry mousse

DINNER

- Steamed baby vegetables with sesame oil
- Glass noodles
- Vanilla cream dessert

HEALTH TIPS

PROTEIN maintains your muscle mass, acts as an appetite suppressant and has a draining effect. And its amino acids keep you calm.

IT'S THE DOSE THAT MATTERS

One serve of protein equals 120–150g lean meat, fish or eggs. Daily dose: half from animal sources, half from plant sources.

Equivalents of 10g protein equal:

- 50g meat or fish • 1 egg • 50g mussels
- 150g cooked white beans
- 120g cooked lentils • 110g wholemeal bread

HERBAL TIP Hawthorn, passion flower, valerian.

THURSDAY

LUNCH

- Tomato with walnut oil
- Pork sautéed with peach
- Wholemeal pilaf
- *Fromage frais* with pepper

DINNER

- Rolled omelette with basil
- Spinach and mushroom salad
- Fruit cocktail with verbena

Winter menus:
zen version

Brrr, now it's cold as well! Maintain your weight and health with good, comforting soups, almost a meal in themselves.

Pulses: a three-bean mix has good GI, fibre and minerals.

BREAKFAST: CHOOSE FROM
- Muesli with sprouted seeds, dried fruit and nuts, hot chocolate made with soy milk
- Milkshake with dried apricots, chestnut cake, spiced tea

MONDAY

LUNCH

- Green salad with diced Gruyère cheese
- Veal with cabbage
- Licorice cream dessert

DINNER

- Cream of carrot soup
- Risotto with chunks of white fish
- Blood orange

TUESDAY

LUNCH

- Black radish
- Turkey sautéed with turnips and honey
- Pink grapefruit

DINNER

- Minestrone
- Clafoutis with pears and ground almonds

Steamed leeks glazed with soy vinegar: beetroot provides a colour contrast.

Rolled veal roast with orange, flavoured with turmeric and wild thyme.

WEDNESDAY

LUNCH
• Chicory (witlof) with granny smith apple
• Cod fillet with turmeric
• Quinoa
• Goat's cheese with walnuts

DINNER
• Gratin of spinach with medium-boiled eggs
• Mandarin

THURSDAY

LUNCH
• Mixed cultivated mushrooms
• Pork cubes with sweet potato and spices
• Crema Catalana with hazelnuts

DINNER
• Borscht with meat
• Rum-flambéed pineapple carpaccio

FRIDAY

LUNCH
• Avocado with soy sauce
• Salmon fricassée
• Julienne of winter vegetables
• Tomme cheese

DINNER
• Three-bean salad
• Italian ham
• Cumin-spiced carrot soufflé
• Dried fruit compote

SATURDAY

LUNCH
• Glazed leeks with beetroot
• Roast veal with orange
• Wholemeal tortellini
• Baked pear

DINNER
• Fish soup with saffron and toasted country bread
• No-pastry tarte Tatin

SUNDAY

LUNCH
• Lamb's lettuce salad with ham and grapes
• Chicken with cider and salsify
• Gratin of mango with coconut

DINNER
• Beef and vegetable casserole
• Plain yoghurt with prunes

Minestrone, the complete soup. Italian cooking at its best.

4

start·your engines

MY ENERGY SOURCE

The right fuel at the right time

Considering our fear of gaining weight, the problem of insulin highs, slow carbs and fast sugars, should we take the glycaemic index with a grain of… sugar?

AN INDEX TO MY WELLBEING? THE WORD FROM NUTRITIONIST DR ARNAUD COCAUL

The glycaemic index (GI) is a guide to the quantity and quality of the sugars (carbohydrates) on our plates. It doesn't concern all foods—meat, for example, doesn't have much effect on blood sugar levels. The GI allows us to compare different foods in terms of how much they raise blood sugar (glucose levels), relative to a benchmark value of 100, which indicates the rate at which the glucose in white bread (or 75g saccharose) is released into the system. Different foods have faster or slower rates of absorption. This means they can be placed in two categories: foods with a **fast** (or high) glycemic index and foods with a **slow** (or low) glycemic index.

BUT WE DON'T EAT FOODS IN ISOLATION

A food with a high GI can be neutralised when eaten within the context of a whole meal—which is why the starter-main-dessert model is much more attractive than a single dish, because there will be a variety of different foods. Then, the mode of preparation (raw or cooked, whole or crushed) will also affect its impact. From a nutritional perspective, the French eating model offers a whole palette of clever GI options.

One of the problems of the glycaemic index is that it demonises certain foods (pasta and white rice)—just as food-combining, Atkins and other 'low carb' diets do. These are then avoided for fear of raising one's blood sugar levels.

WE THINK WE NEED TO AVOID STARCH TO LOSE WEIGHT

… and suddenly it's all we can think about! **A terrible deprivation and for good reason: the brain is the number one consumer of sugar** (it uses almost half of the glucose we consume).

THE WORD FROM THE DIETITIAN
Hyperglycaemic: GI of 70+
- dates
- french bread and sandwich bread
- rice cakes
- cooked potatoes, potato mash, potato chips
- cornflakes
- white rice

Medium GI: GI of 55 – 70
- basmati rice
- wholemeal, sourdough and wholegrain breads
- sweetcorn
- soy and soy-based products
- saccharose

Low GI: GI 55
- wholemeal pasta
- natural muesli
- black bread and stone-ground wholemeal bread
- apples
- lentils, white beans, chickpeas, green peas
- oranges

SCIENCE NOTE
The consumption of glucose is a relatively recent phenomenon. Prior to the industrialisation of agriculture, our system was used to a low-GI diet: roots, tubers, plants, whole or unpeeled fruits.

Chestnuts with star anise (very effective against bloating) and other spices.

Menus
to warm up winter

Calories with a purpose, and energy to burn: the plan to beat the chill starts with good fats and low-GI starches— dishes that (also) warm your heart.

BREAKFAST: CHOOSE FROM
- Toast with a little butter, watermelon jam and walnuts, orange juice, ginger tea
- Kiwifruit and fresh curd cheese with nuts, buckwheat crispbread, coffee

MONDAY

LUNCH
- Lamb tagine with pumpkin
- Couscous with raisins
- Pineapple compote with cinnamon

DINNER
- Cumin-spiced lentil soup
- Cheese soufflé with nutmeg
- Endive with cider vinegar
- Banana mousse

TUESDAY

LUNCH
- Grated carrot
- Monkfish medallion with ginger
- Rice
- Pears with chocolate

DINNER
- Onion soup (with gratin topping)
- Baked eggs with spinach in béchamel sauce
- Spiced chestnuts with star anise

WEDNESDAY

LUNCH
- Tarama-filled chicory (witlof)
- Sautéed veal with salsify
- Dates

DINNER
- Mixed vegetable soup with pistou
- Pot-braised cabbage with bacon
- Gratin of seasonal fruit

A right pear: the comfort of chocolate

Laurence Salomon's tofu mille-feuille with spinach (recipe page 190).

The deliciously pervasive perfume of cumin: a tagine of slow-cooked onions and dried summer fruits.

FRIDAY

LUNCH
- Shredded celery dressed with balsamic vinegar
- Laurence Salomon's tofu mille-feuille with spinach, rice and orange emulsion (recipe page 190)
- Fresh goat's cheese

DINNER
- Rustic tomato soup
- Gratin of rutabaga with ham
- Kiwifruit with almonds

SATURDAY

LUNCH
- Red cabbage salad
- Old-fashioned beef stew with turnips and carrots
- Rum-and-raisin ramekin

DINNER
- Savoy-style cheese fondue
- Fruit salad with hazelnuts and prunes

SUNDAY

LUNCH
- Duck *pot au feu*
- Mulled spice wine
- Walnut shortbread

DINNER
- Leek and potato soup
- Sauté of baby mushrooms
- Vanilla custard cream

THURSDAY

LUNCH
- Curly endive salad with walnuts
- Chicken curry with pineapple and coconut milk
- Reblochon cheese

DINNER
- Cod fillets with paprika
- Steamed potatoes
- Apples with honey

HEALTH TIPS

TURMERIC
A concentrated dose of health benefits, not only anti-ageing, but anti-bacterial, anti-viral, and anti-inflammatory. Use it against the winter germs that lurk around us. Its light, delicate flavour works well with meat, fish, vegetables and grains, and its golden colour shines out from the plate, even on the cloudiest days.

DRIED FRUITS
Especially grapes, which neutralise the acidity of our system.

Multicoloured soup: put dried beans on the menu two or three times a week.

Oily fish are welcome at the table throughout the season.

Menus for a tip-top summer

Stay dynamic… whatever the temperature. Walking, gym exercise, swimming, cycling… jump at every opportunity to get moving.

BREAKFAST: CHOOSE FROM
• Dried fruit compote, yoghurt or *fromage blanc*, buckwheat flakes, Earl Grey tea
• Seasonal fruits, almond or soy milk and rolled oats, green tea
• Boiled egg, wholemeal bread, hazelnut butter, coffee

Oat biscuits: simple to make and low GI as well.

TUESDAY
LUNCH
• Marinated green and red capsicum (pepper)
• Rolled escalope of chicken with green peas
• Nectarines
DINNER
• Quinoa casserole with baby summer vegetables
• Roquefort cheese

Quinoa with sun-soaked vegetables: a marriage made in heaven, bursting with protein and vitamins.

MONDAY
LUNCH
• Grated carrot with ginger
• Salmon fillet with poppyseeds and two kinds of lentil
• Berry tiramisù
DINNER
• Potato and eggplant (aubergine) bake with pine nuts
• Rhubarb compote

WEDNESDAY
LUNCH
• Tomato with French shallot
• Grilled bream with dill
• Wholemeal rice with turmeric
• Raspberry mousse
DINNER
• Gratin of fennel with fresh curd cheese
• Little oat biscuits with raisins

THURSDAY

LUNCH

• Terrine of goat's cheese
with beetroot

• Braised veal

• Mille-feuille of zucchini
(courgette) with wild thyme

• Figs

DINNER

• White bean and savoury casserole

• Cherry and redcurrant soup

*Cooking tomatoes and the addition
of fat or oil boosts their dose of lycopene.*

FRIDAY

LUNCH

• Batavia lettuce with walnuts

• Grilled beef salad with soy sauce
and sesame seeds, basmati rice

• Blackcurrant ice cream

DINNER

• Curried barley with tomatoes
and capsicum (pepper)

• Peaches with mint

HEALTH TIPS

Be inspired by the **RAINBOW METHOD**: professor David Heber classifies fruits and vegetables into seven colour groups: Red/Purple, Red, Orange, Orange/Yellow, White/Green, Yellow/Green, Green. Work through every shade, in matte, shiny or high-gloss versions for multicoloured meals.
GINSENG This vital energy (Qi) tonic in Chinese medicine improves physical and mental ability and adaptability to stress. The word 'ginseng' means 'man-shaped essence of the earth'.

SATURDAY

LUNCH

• Fresh red radish salad

• Dill-stuffed sardines

• Spiced eggplant (aubergine)

• Melon and watermelon
with green tea

DINNER

• Mexican salad with corn
and red kidney beans

• Plum clafoutis

SUNDAY

LUNCH

• Mango, radicchio and rocket
(arugula) salad

• Duck breast grilled skin-side down

• Green beans

• Golden delicious apple and tomato tart

DINNER

• Mackerel fillets marinated
with crushed garlic

• Steamed potatoes

• Fresh curd cheese with strawberries

Golden caramelised roast pork with thyme, an anti-viral and anti-bacterial herb.

Menus
for recuperation

Protein provides the essential amino acids (our body can't make them) needed for the synthesis of muscle proteins.

BREAKFAST: CHOOSE FROM
- Wholemeal bread, slice of ham, orange, coffee
- Wholegrain bread, boiled egg, fruit salad with almonds
- Wholemeal bread, hazelnut butter, lemon tea
- Wholegrain cereal, prunes and hazelnuts, soy yoghurt, black tea

TUESDAY

LUNCH
- Chicory (witlof) with kiwifruit and sesame seeds
- *Boudin noir* with apple
- Potato purée with nutmeg
- Salad of oranges and pomelos

DINNER
- Breton-style fish soup
- Semolina pudding with stewed fruit

WEDNESDAY

LUNCH
- White cabbage in a remoulade sauce
- Chicken escalope with cream
- Rice pilaf
- Cinnamon-spiced poached meringue with crème anglaise

DINNER
- Salmon and leek lasagne
- Blackcurrant compote

MONDAY

LUNCH
- Artichoke hearts in olive oil
- Pan-fried zucchini (courgette) with salmon
- Wholemeal bread
- Farmhouse tomme cheese

DINNER
- French shepherd's pie with carrot purée
- Raspberry tart

Grapefruit with peel and pith removed, with orange, vanilla and orange flower water.

THURSDAY

LUNCH
- Green salad with corn
- Hungarian-style goulash
- Wholemeal tagliatelle
- Comté cheese

DINNER
- Scrambled eggs with baby spinach
- Steamed diced celery
- Fruit salad of pears with hazelnuts

Small artichokes with the heart to help eliminate bad fats.

FRIDAY

LUNCH

- Beetroot
- Roast pork with herbs
- Lentils with mustard
- Bulgarian yoghurt with cherry jam

DINNER

- Broccoli soup
- Buckwheat pancakes with cheese
- Green salad
- Apricot mousse

SATURDAY

LUNCH

- Steamed fennel with a lemon vinaigrette
- Fish tagine with raisins and sweet potato
- Mixed fruit salad with orange flower water

DINNER

- Chinese cabbage rolls stuffed with cumin-spiced beef mince
- Sheep's milk yoghurt with sweet chestnut purée

HEALTH TIPS

THE LOW-DOWN ON CARBS
Our system is better adapted to low-GI foods (tubers, plants and pulses, whole or unpeeled fruit). Starch is made up of amylose (low-GI) and amylopectin (high-GI). Refined grains are higher in amylopectin: basmati rice is one that contains more amylose.
BOUDIN NOIR This is very high in **IRON** (which can be low during menstruation). You can boost its absorption by adding **VITAMIN C**, so bring on the oranges and kiwifruit. But remember that this vitamin is sensitive to light and heat: cooking destroys most of it.
HERBAL TIP Blackcurrant has anti-inflammatory, anti-oxidant and analgesic properties. Dose up!

For a quick version, you can just add frozen fish and seafood to a bisque-style soup.

SUNDAY

LUNCH

- Fresh avocado and prawn cocktail
- Steak with French shallots
- Italian-style flat (runner) beans
- Walnut and cinnamon cake

DINNER

- Carrot and coriander (cilantro) soup
- Hard-boiled eggs stuffed with sardines and capers
- Praline-flavoured dessert

Menus
to beat the blues

Good dietary sources of omega-3 are essential for wellbeing and the smooth functioning of our neurotransmitters: we need them to stimulate the production of serotonin. Have some music playing while you eat, and don't forget to breathe and to smile!

BREAKFAST: CHOOSE FROM
- Wholemeal walnut bread, fresh fruit salad, almond butter, rose-scented tea
- Half a pomelo, rolled oats, soy milk, hazelnuts and crushed (in the coffee grinder) linseeds, dried apricots

---

Red, yellow, orange and green capsicums (peppers): one of the best vegetable sources of beta carotene.

TUESDAY

LUNCH
- Poached cod with vegetables and canola-oil aïoli
- Fresh pineapple with cashew nuts

DINNER
- Minestrone with pistou
- Sheep's milk cheese with cherry preserve

WEDNESDAY

LUNCH
- Carrots cooked with sesame seeds
- Calf liver with onions and white wine
- Yellow beans
- Vanilla crème brûlée

DINNER
- Wholemeal spaghetti with mussels and parsley
- Prunes

MONDAY

LUNCH
- Lamb's lettuce salad with crab
- Pork with lime and fenugreek
- Brown rice
- Chocolate *fondant*

DINNER
- Gratin of silverbeet (Swiss chard) with garlic and anchovies
- Flambéed bananas

Chocolatissimo: 70 per cent cocoa, not much sugar, hardly any butter… Maximum flavour!

THURSDAY

LUNCH

- Broccoli vinaigrette with pinenuts
- Escabeche of sardines
- Quinoa pilaf
- Yoghurt with acacia honey

DINNER

- Two kinds of capsicum filled with spinach rice
- Kiwifruit

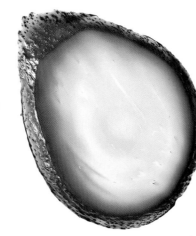

Avocado: always a good advocate for health, with nothing but good fats.

FRIDAY

LUNCH

- Avocado and tomato guacamole
- Chicken with exotic spices and ginger
- Baked eggplant (aubergine)
- Gruyère cheese

DINNER

- Mackerel paté
- Purple potato salad
- Cinnamon-poached pear

Goat's cheese: the cheese with the lowest fat content. Choose raw-milk, farmhouse versions.

SATURDAY

LUNCH

- Beetroot with mustard sauce
- Niçoise-style beef stew with herbs
- Burghul with semi-dried tomatoes
- Goat's cheese with French-style gingerbread

DINNER

- Red lentil casserole with baby vegetables
- Date and orange salad

Crustaceans raise serotonin levels.

SUNDAY

LUNCH

- Oysters with lemon and pepper
- Grilled king prawn kebab
- Rice
- Berry crumble with hazelnuts

DINNER

- Pumpkin soup
- Eggs with Scandinavian-style herring
- Braised spinach
- Baked apple

HEALTH TIPS

LOST YOUR TASTE FOR LIFE?

It's not simply an expression: we will soon be able to detect depression thanks to a saliva test… If you can no longer tell the difference between salty and sweet (at very low levels), it's a sign you're depressed! **HERBAL TIP**: St John's wort (to be used with caution).

Berry crumble with granola.

5 anti-age

MY REJUVENATION SOURCE

Operation antioxidant

What causes us to age? Life-giving oxygen which becomes an enemy and attacks vital components of our system. Fortunately, antioxidants are there to help! Nutritionist Dr Arnaud Cocaul explains.

OXYGEN, THE ENEMY OF YOUTH: TO BREATHE IS TO AGE

What ages us is oxygen, which is vital of course, turning traitor by becoming a poison: each breath is 'killing us softly' by generating **free radicals,** which cause the oxidisation that ages our cells. Fortunately, our body has a solution: **integrated antioxidant systems**. The **mitochondria**, our cell's power plants, are there to serve as safeguards by eliminating oxidisation. The only problem is that, over time, the enzyme repair system tires out, the cells' powers of recuperation becomes less effective and our DNA ends up deteriorating. The stage is set for the process of degenerative disease.

Oxidative stress is all of these oxidising agents that are internally generated (endogenous oxidative stress), but can also be connected to external factors (exogenous oxidative stress): tobacco, stress, hypertension, exposure to sun and pollution. Against these threats, our skin is obviously in the front line. Hence the need to protect it from free radicals from the outside, but also the inside: in this sense, healthy nutrition and dermatology work hand in hand. **Zinc, selenium and glutathione** will fight, on the level of the skin, the damage of A and B ultraviolet rays.

EAT YOURSELF YOUNG

To neutralise free radicals, there are two clear courses of action: minimise the sources of damage (from tobacco to UV rays) and increase your levels of antioxidants. Hence the importance of eating less meat (as meat raises stress) and **varying your diet so that you're not always coming up against the same kind of oxidisation**.

We're gaining three months every year!
Life expectancy is at a high rate of inflation: increasing by 30 years over 100 years… And since 1935, we know, thanks to Clive McCay and his experiments on rats, that eating less offers direct benefits for our longevity.

THE WORD FROM THE EXPERT
Eat less to live more. Calorie restriction can ease oxidative stress on muscle cells, according to the conclusions of a study conducted by researchers at the Pennington Biomedical Research Center.

Radically anti-radical

Once we've eliminated the causes of oxidative stress, all that's left is to become best buddies with known and acknowledged anti-ageing champions.

FRUITS AND VEGETABLES: PROTECTIVE FIBRE

Roots or tubers, leaves or stems, shoots or flowers, they throw their whole bodies into the cause.

FLAVONOIDS, POLYPHENOLS, FOLATES AND RESVERATROL: PUBLIC ENEMIES NUMBER ONE OF OXIDATIVE STRESS

A healthy diet has the same effect as anti-ageing medicines, without the risks or side effects. Many scientists attest to the antioxidant effect of polyphenols in fruits, vegetables, red wine and green tea, against free radicals, the origin of cell ageing. The thousands of antioxidants contained in plant-based foods let the plant protect itself from free radicals. In us, they help in the prevention of chronic illnesses and slow down the ageing process.

COLOUR WHEEL: THE ANTIOXIDANT PALETTE

- **reds, yellows and oranges** (capsicums [peppers], apples, tomatoes, citrus fruit, peaches, carrots): contain **carotenoids, lycopene** and **lutein**.
- **purples and violets** (red cabbage, beetroot, figs, prunes, dark grapes, blackberries, blackcurrants): contain **anthocyanin**.
- **greens** (lettuces, spinach, cabbage): contain **chlorophyll**.

The top 10 antioxidant foods (source: Mayo Clinic)
- almonds
- broccoli
- spinach
- wheat germ
- vegetable juice
- red kidney beans
- bilberries (European blueberries)
- sweet potato
- apple
- salmon

THE NUTRITIONIST'S FAVOURITES
Blackcurrant, cranberry and walnuts.

Omega megastars

Essential for brain function, the benefits of omega essential fatty acids are sung far and wide.

OMEGA-6 OR -3?

More than 60 per cent of our brain is made up of lipids, more than 70 per cent of which are omega-3s. Because fats are formed from different fatty acids (numbered according to codes that are linked to the biochemical configuration of the molecule), a good balance between them is essential for maintaining good health.

Omega-3s keep their promises

Their role in protecting against cardiovascular illnesses has been established, and there is speculation regarding degenerative illness. But increasing levels of omega-3 is only useful if at the same time you lower levels of omega-6, which we consume, in the form of sunflower oil. Fortunately, more and more commercial producers are now turning to canola oil.

THE RIGHT PROPORTIONS

The maximum daily intake is five times more omega-6s than omega-3s, whereas we currently consume (on average) 10 times more, or twice as much as we should! We need to reduce the percentage of **saturated fatty acids** on our plates (fatty meats, deli meats, pastries, baked items, cheeses), and put the brakes on the omega-6 **polyunsaturated fatty acids**, such as sunflower oil (omega-6s are already very common in mass-produced foods, some margarines and biscuits).

Feast on **monounsaturated fatty acids**: the most famous one, olive oil (also called omega-9), and, above all, the **polyunsaturated omega-3 fatty acids**: canola, linseed and oily fish.

THE WORD FROM THE EXPERT

Two polyunsaturated fatty acids are said to be 'essential', because our body doesn't know how to make them:
• an omega-6, linoleic acid (found in corn and sunflower oil)
• an omega-3, alpha-linolenic acid (canola, linseed, walnut oil). Our enzymes enable the transformation of this alpha-linolenic acid into other fatty acids, still omega-3s, but with a slightly different structure: EPA (eicosapentaenoic acid) and DHA (docosahexaenoic acid). These anti-inflammatories regularise our blood parameters, improve cardiovascular health and are indispensable to the nervous system and our mental wellbeing. They are found directly in this form in oily fish.

Baby milk formulas

These are said to be too high in omega-6s and not high enough in saturated fatty acids (unlike breast milk).

Crete and Okinawa: treasure islands

Micronutrients, maximum effects: revisiting the two star traditional diets for genuine rejuvenation therapy.

THE ISLANDS WHERE OLD AGE IS NOT A SHIPWRECK

Of course, the locals have a healthy lifestyle, share a certain outlook on life and benefit from strong social ties. But this still doesn't explain why there is so little cardiovascular illness on Crete… but the **quality of fats** consumed there does.

As for the archipelago of Okinawa, located to the south of Japan, it is celebrated for its incredible concentration of fighting-fit centenarians: 15 per cent of the world's population aged over 110 live there!

WHAT THEIR DIETS HAVE IN COMMON

- low calorie intake
- lots of fruits and vegetables that are high in fibre, vitamins and mineral salts
- fish and crustaceans, which are high in omega-3s
- low intake of meat

What they eat on Crete… but not on Okinawa

- bread
- cheese (a little!)
- olives and olive oil
- red wine (a glass a day, preferably at lunchtime)

What they eat on Okinawa… but not on Crete

- sweet potato
- spices (turmeric, ginger, galangal, cinnamon)
- seaweed
- soy-based products

Wise up
On one of the beaches in Okinawa, this engraving can be read on a rock: "At 70, you are just a child, at 80, barely an adolescent, and at 90, if the ancestors invite you up to heaven, ask them to wait until you're 100, when you'll reconsider the issue."

The butterfly-effect: pasta with seafood and rocket (arugula).

My menus:
Cretan-style

The Cretan diet is very beneficial for the cardiovascular system: fresh fruit and vegetables, bread, grains, a little wine, more fish than meat, olive oil and a little cheese.

> **BREAKFAST: CHOOSE FROM**
> • Wholewheat bread, a little butter (or olive oil for the adventurous), fresh fruits, coffee
> • Greek-style sheep's milk yoghurt, honey, fresh figs, almonds, green tea

MONDAY

LUNCH
• Chickpeas with olive oil
• Veal escalope
• Eggplant (aubergine) purée
• Muscat grapes

DINNER
• Garlic soup
• Tomato stuffed with goat's cheese and green olives
• Peaches with mint

TUESDAY

LUNCH
• Purslane with hazelnut oil
• Chicken with lemon and garlic
• Steamed green beans
• Watermelon

DINNER
• Pumpkin soup
• Mediterranean vegetable and potato bake
• *Fromage frais*

WEDNESDAY

LUNCH
• Lamb's lettuce with walnuts and balsamic vinegar
• Mackerel in white wine with steamed fennel
• Apricots

DINNER
• Zucchini (courgette) and goat's cheese mille-feuille
• Pear poached in cinnamon-spiced wine

THURSDAY

LUNCH
• Artichoke vinaigrette
• Seafood and rocket (arugula)
• Apple mousse with almonds

DINNER
• Scrambled eggs with chanterelle mushrooms
• Mixed salad with sheep's milk cheese

Gently sautéed chanterelle mushrooms. All mushrooms provide carbohydrates, mineral salts (they are high in potassium) and precious carotenoids.

*Symbols of the good life,
Cretan-style.*

FRIDAY

LUNCH

- Lentil salad
- Rabbit roasted with thyme
- Kohlrabi with walnuts
and black olives
- Tea-soaked prunes

DINNER

- Spinach rice
- Lettuce
- Strawberries with lemon

SATURDAY

LUNCH

- Tomato with feta cheese
- Sardines with grilled capsicum
- Wholegrain rice pilaf
- Macerated fruit salad

DINNER

- White beans with carrots
and savoury
- Melon

SUNDAY

LUNCH

- Black radish
- Baked snails with tarragon
- Steamed potatoes
- Roasted figs with a fruit coulis

DINNER

- French garlic soup
- Rye toast with tapenade
and anchovies
- Curly endive
- Plum compote

*Sardines (so-called because of
Sardinia, a neighbouring island)
provide protein and omega-3s, and
are sublime combined with capsicum,
grilled so they can be easily peeled.*

*The fig, a thing of wonder,
raw or cooked.*

A wok makes last-minute cooking possible by quickly combining all the ingredients.

My menus:
Okinawa-style

A little more difficult to put into practice than the Cretan diet, but so varied and full of flavours… An everyday pleasure and long-term insurance!

BREAKFAST: CHOOSE FROM
• Green tea with lemon, rice semolina with soy milk, hazelnut butter, banana
• Green tea with ginger, sweet potato cake (recipe opposite), raisins, kiwifruit
• Green tea with jasmine, flaked buckwheat with soy milk, cinnamon-spiced apple compote

MONDAY

LUNCH

• Miso soup with wakame

• Halibut cooked *en papillote*

• Fennel with thyme

• Carrot cake

DINNER

• Avocado and cucumber sushi rolls

• Soy yoghurt with bilberries

(European blueberries)

TUESDAY

LUNCH

• White cabbage salad

• Chicken curry with turmeric

and ginger

• Basmati rice with poppyseeds

• Soy ice cream with blackcurrant

DINNER

• Grilled sardines with lemon

• Small buckwheat pancakes with

diced zucchini (courgette)

• Pear and macadamia nuts

Sushi rolls, with seaweed and rice, then let your imagination run free: a small canvas you can learn to master.

A line-up of all the star ingredients from Okinawa.

HEALTH TIPS

THE SEAWEEDS

Wakame, kombu, dulse, sea lettuce, nori (for sushi rolls), spirulina. They provide trace elements, the same amount of mineral salts and vitamins as vegetables, and essential fatty acids. They are becoming increasingly widely available, in various forms. Dried seaweeds are rehydrated to add to soups, salads or vegetable dishes, and added to fish at the end of cooking.

SWEET POTATO CAKES

Sweet potato cakes, for breakfast? It's child's play. Steam and mash 2 sweet potatoes, add 3 egg yolks, a little brown sugar, ground almonds, and the egg white beaten into peaks. Form into patties and bake in a moderate oven for 30 minutes.

THURSDAY

LUNCH

- Raw grated beetroot with raspberry vinegar
- Sushi of mackerel and bream
- Baked apple with almond butter

DINNER

- Scrambled eggs with broccoli
- Red quinoa
- Grapefruit

FRIDAY

LUNCH

- Cod liver
- Wok-fried pork with Chinese cabbage
- Exotic fruit salad with papaya

DINNER

- Glass noodles with mussels and calamari
- Tapioca pudding

SATURDAY

LUNCH

- Grilled tuna and sesame oil
- Purple rice with shiitake mushrooms
- Soy yoghurt and diced pineapple

DINNER

- Pork salad with three kinds of capsicum (pepper)
- Milkshake of almond milk with raspberries

SUNDAY

LUNCH

- Grated black radish
- Duck tenderloins with walnuts and pomegranate
- Curried pea purée
- Lemon sorbet with verbena

DINNER

- Sweet potato sautéed with pumpkin and raisins
- Soufflé omelette with coconut milk and roasted pineapple

Soufflé omelette with roasted pineapple.

WEDNESDAY

LUNCH

- Watercress salad with sesame seeds
- Dogfish with onion and galangal
- Rice pudding with peach compote

DINNER

- Baby vegetables stir-fried with tofu
- Dark chocolate with orange peel

6

thirsting for a detox

MY PURITY SOURCE

Detox without the brainwash

Going to extremes is, by definition, a mistake.
Are you aiming for a good conscience via self-flagellation
or scare tactics? There is the naturopath's point of view.

THE WORD FROM LAURENCE SALOMON, CHEF AND NATUROPATH

If you eat well, why would you need to go on a course of detoxification? It just legitimises overindulgence: you should be wary of detox diets. Once you have a healthy diet—which is in no way synonymous with depressing food or being 'on' a diet, but on the contrary means harmony and wellbeing—what's the use of these punishing periods of pseudo-purification?

YOU DON'T *'INTOX'* YOURSELF WHEN YOU EAT!

Food is not an enemy. If it's chosen well and is as little processed and messed around with as possible, it's a source of life—meant to become a living part of ourselves. As for waste products, they are made up of the fibre in food that we can't digest and the shedding of the colonic membrane (it's the only organ that undergoes so much regeneration).

Regretting a period of overindulgence? The obvious solution: reduce quantities.

Moderation is the golden rule. Even the best food, in excessive quantities, ages our organs. Digestion fatigues our body—hence the damage caused by snacking.

My detox prescription

Avoid fasting and 'mono' diets, instead find a happy medium.

Japanese-style
• An evening bowl of rice and miso soup: slow carbs for the night and the broth to hydrate.

Express detox
• Two or three glasses of magnesium chloride (the sachets dissolve in a glass of water) for a gentle intestinal flush.
• 'Derivative bath' therapy (helps to drain toxins towards the intestines and pelvis).

Long-term detox
Drink kombucha 'tea', a powerful probiotic because it's alive: it's not dehydrated or freeze-dried and it passes very easily through the stomach barrier. Kombucha, a 'long-life' mushroom, is fermented in sweetened tea, which it turns into lactic acid. It's a real vitamin drink that rebalances the intestinal flora.

Foods with detox fibre
• apple • kiwifruit • avocado
• artichoke • garlic • beetroot
• cabbage • prune • seaweed
• watercress • birch juice

The Palaeolithic diet: going back to square one

The incredible success of the 'caveman' diet demands that we ponder the question: what can we possibly learn from the habits of our hunter-gatherer ancestors?

WHY DOES IT WORK?

While our species is seven million years old, our genes haven't evolved as quickly as our environment. Human beings used to eat plants (leaves, tubers, roots), meat and eggs, fish and shellfish. The search for food used up a lot of energy. It was a very vitamin-rich diet. Ten thousand years ago the rearing of animals and agriculture altered these habits, with the introduction of dairy products, fattier meat and grains. Then the Industrial Revolution and the development of the agri-food industry made a more diverse range of food available. Today, **the excess of dairy products and gluten (wheat)** is increasingly implicated in various intolerances, allergies and inflammations.

HOW SHOULD WE RESPOND? SIMPLY BY EATING MORE

Eat more:

• lean meat: our ancestors ate well-muscled game meats

• crustaceans, shellfish

• all fresh fruit and vegetables, roots, tubers

• dried fruit and nuts

• pulses.

THE WORD FROM THE DIETITIAN
It's not a matter of eliminating all wheat or dairy-based mass-produced foods, but of returning to a more natural diet by changing (bad) habits: that is, eat less refined grains, processed foods, saturated fats, cooked food, salt and sugar.

My menus: Palaeolithically correct

Coconut: a ball of explosive energy.

Not very tempting at first glance, but as soon as you try it your whole being will thank you: a guaranteed improvement in your wellbeing in just a few days.

BREAKFAST
• Meadowsweet tea, hard-boiled egg, chestnut-flour polenta, fresh fruits

MONDAY

LUNCH
• Carpaccio of boletus mushrooms with red cabbage
• Sauté of boar (or pork) with chestnuts and broad (fava) beans
• Pear

DINNER
• Pumpkin soup
• Seafood *persillade* (seasoned with chopped garlic and parsley)
• Grapefruit

TUESDAY

LUNCH
• Reindeer (or beef) tartare
• White bean stew
• Apricot kebabs

DINNER
• Soft-boiled eggs
• Green asparagus
• Honey-glazed hazelnuts

WEDNESDAY

LUNCH
• Salmon tartare with pink grapefruit and avocado
• Steamed zucchini (courgette) with walnut oil
• Plums

DINNER
• Sorrel soup
• Frog's legs
• Cumin-spiced carrot
• Pineapple

Apricot kebab, skewered on a vanilla pod.

THURSDAY

LUNCH
• Watercress salad
• Calf liver fricassée with brussels sprouts
• Poached apple with lingonberries

DINNER
• Casserole of snails with fennel and thyme
• Dates

Game makes for a tasty meal.

SUNDAY

LUNCH

- Dandelion salad
- Quails with turnips
- Red berries

DINNER

- Mussels with French shallot and saffron
- Gently stewed leek
- Orange and almonds

Grilled fish equals flavour.

Raw foods, a real health parade.

FRIDAY

LUNCH

- Radicchio
- Mixed grilled fish
- Spinach rice
- Cashews

DINNER

- Rabbit with onions
- Sautéed Jerusalem artichokes
- Kiwifruit

SATURDAY

LUNCH

- Ostrich steak with wild thyme
- Salsify with sage
- Coconut cream dessert

DINNER

- Omelette with wild mushrooms
- Lamb's lettuce with linseed
- Banana

HEALTH TIPS

VITAMIN C: IT'S THE DOSE THAT MATTERS

Only primates, certain bats and guinea pigs aren't able to synthesise vitamin C from glucose. The gene hasn't appeared for millions of years: perhaps because of a period of abundance? The French Food Safety Agency recommends 110mg per day; Linus Pauling, Nobel Prize winner and patron saint of vitamin C, recommended 200mg!

My beauty is nourished by the moisture in my body

The hydration equation:
thirst no more

In our body's irrigation system, thirst performs its role as an anti-dehydration alarm system. Note: the benefits of drinking water in high doses are no longer as clear-cut as you might have thought.

Beautiful morning
As soon as you wake up, drink a glass of water at body temperature: a habit that gently rehydrates the system and eliminates toxins accumulated during the night, especially in the intestine.

THE WORD FROM THE NUTRITIONIST
The recommended daily intake of 1.5 litres has been put in question by a study in the *Journal of the American Society of Nephrology*. A large percentage of the water we need to restore our 'water balance' is provided by food. All foods contain water, except sugar and oil. The higher the fat content of a food, the lower its water content. There is:
- 95 per cent water in green lettuce
- 91 per cent in a tomato
- 89 per cent in a carrot
- 75 per cent in meat, fish and shellfish
- 35 per cent in bread
- 5 per cent in peanuts.

LIQUID CURRENCY

Our 50,000 billion cells are bathed in 2.5–3 litres of water that are renewed daily. But dehydration only poses a real threat, in our climate, to babies and the elderly, who are not or no longer able to perceive the sensation of thirst. Even if you're no longer devoted to the regimen of the regulation litre and a half (see side bar), you mustn't neglect **thirst signals** or your bodily wellbeing.

Water remains the undisputed king of 'health' drinks (and the only food we all must have), with a total of zero calories (as long as it's unflavoured) and, in the case of natural mineral waters (the only waters whose composition is guaranteed), a provider of beneficial mineral salts, with calcium and magnesium at the top of the list. But these waters also contribute to our spreading carbon footprint due to billions of plastic bottles. Unfiltered or not (the filtration jugs do a good job), tap water remains the most environmentally-friendly solution.

DRINKING DOESN'T MELT OFF WEIGHT…

No more than it's true that you shouldn't drink at mealtimes: on the contrary, drinking while you eat helps you digest. But it's logical to drink more when you're eating less, because you're obviously not getting as much hydration from food.

THE NATUROPATH'S RECOMMENDATION

Hydrate with small sips, don't force yourself to drink big glassfuls. Drinking opens the floodgates: the less you drink the less you get thirsty—and vice versa.

Judicious juices!

The pure benefits of juices are extolled in health circles, but it's their sugar content that poses a problem.

A JUICY MARKET

From orange juice (always the market leader), with its extra multivitamins, to the astringency of polyphenol-stuffed red berries, **fruit juices are enjoying huge popularity.**

BOTTLED JUICE: NO ADDED SUGAR

Even so: not only will juice contain more calories and not be as satisfying than a whole fruit, but these drinks are full of fast sugars. Be careful: only those marked 100 per cent pure juice are guaranteed to contain any fruit!

SYRUPS, SMOOTHIES AND CO.

Products evolve along with expectations. Alongside the traditional juices, smoothies—closer to desserts—are quietly taking the upper hand.

A GOOD SQUEEZE

Remember: fruits and vegetables lose their fibre in the juice extractor. Which means they also lose some of their good properties… but this allows sensitive digestive tracts to absorb them raw—and gradually get used to them.

TOMATOES AND CARROTS: VEGETABLES GET INTO THE ACT

Yes to vitamin-rich cocktails! Note that some gazpacho-style preparations can be high in fat.

Soft drink versus juice: which has more sugar?

A litre of soft drink contains the equivalent of 20 sugar cubes and up to 450 calories. What can top that? Fruit juices and smoothies! A litre contains on average 480 calories.

THE WORD FROM THE NUTRITIONIST

Liquids don't fill you up: after a smoothie, you eat just as much at the next meal! The instant feeling of fullness disappears as quickly as it arrives, prompting hypoglycemia, the by-product of the insulin high. As a snack, it's better to combine it with something solid.

Let's break for coffee... or tea?

Our favourite natural stimulants are taking on new virtues. Here are some new revelations on the fortifying powers of these two exceptional beverages which keep us company from the moment we wake up.

TEA: HAVE IT PLAIN OR WITH LEMON

The magic powers of tea, due to its flavonoid content, are supposed to be completely nullified as soon as you add a drop of milk! An experiment conducted at the Charité medical school in Berlin showed that the casein in milk prevented the catechins from having their effect on the vascular level. As for milky coffee, often difficult to digest, it's not recommended as an everyday drink.

THE WORD FROM THE EXPERT
COFFEE AGAINST ALZHEIMER'S

Researchers at the French National Institute for Health and Medical Research have shown that drinking three cups of coffee per day preserves the mental abilities of women above 65. It's a discovery supported by the *Journal of Neuroinflammation*: by protecting the brain against excess levels of cholesterol it minimises the risk of dementia.

CAFFEINE AND THEINE: THE SAME KICK?

It's the same molecule under two different names... But there's still more caffeine in coffee than in tea. Our favourite natural stimulants act through similar means: the alkaloids.

Smell the coffee: caffeine gathers up sources of energy and prolongs resistance to fatigue, but its phenolic compounds also happen to be particularly effective antioxidants. Unsurpassed when it comes to **concentration**, coffee also works as a memory-aid (see left)... Once again, it's the dose that matters!

TEA GETS THE GREEN LIGHT

There's caffeine in tea, but also theophylline (a vasodilator) and theobromine (a diuretic). Among the various teas, black tea has 10 times less catechins (the flavonoids that, among other things, affect weight loss) than **green tea**. Whether it's Japanese tea, from the tonic sencha or matcha (with 70 times more antioxidants than orange juice) to the Chinese yunnan (a diuretic) and gunpowder teas (best combined with mint), we delight in their **polyphenols**. Four or more cups a day lowers glycaemia and suppresses oxidative stress. Tea is also able to counter bad cholesterol and lower the risk of cardiovascular disease and stroke. It helps digestion and limits the absorption of fats, especially around the waist. One of its polyphenols (epigallocatechin gallate) is an object of research in relation to tumour growth.

Wining, like dining: in moderation

No-one today doubts wine's paradoxical benefits. Red wine can now boast about its health benefits… on the strict condition you don't go over your recommended dose.

TANNIN: ALL BETS ON THE RED

UNCORKED: THE RESVERATROL REVELATION

In small doses, wine can be beneficial for your health, according to nutritional specialists, including Dr Jean-Michel Lecerf. This is thanks to the variety of polyphenols it contains: a complex group of molecules with proven antioxidant and anti-coagulant properties. Not only does it not increase the risk of obesity or diabetes, it has protective effects against cardiovascular disease through its effect on good cholesterol and its ability to limit clot formation in the arteries.

Between one and two glasses per day (the maximum dose for a woman) represents a good form of life insurance. Above this, not only do you multiply the risk of alcohol dependency, but the 'empty' calories provide extra kilos.

THE WORD FROM NATUROPATH CHEF, LAURENCE SALOMON

"I only serve **natural wines**, made from grapes that are grown organically, which is to say using as few chemicals as possible—we absorb amounts of pesticides in wines where the grapes, having been sprayed with multiple chemicals, are crushed without being washed. Producing natural wines is a global approach from the vine through to the wine-making process, producing unsulfured wines (apart from very low amounts in whites and rosés), which are much more digestible, with a striking flavour in the mouth where the fruit is at the forefront. Since **resveratrol** is the vine's defence mechanism against parasites, the more it is chemically treated, the less it will have."

Champagne

A little lower in calories (80 calories per 100g) than red or white wine (90 calories), it is also lower in alcohol (10 per cent rather than 12 or 13). But its bubbles go to the head more quickly. The result: you drink less and get more drunk. Thinking of a cider or beer? They're supposed to be probiotics. In small doses!

ZERO ALCOHOL WHEN PREGNANT

An increasingly justifiable precautionary measure. The damaging effects of alcohol on the unborn baby are unanimously confirmed by studies. As for breastfeeding, to the extent that alcohol is expressed in the milk, it's best to be prudent.

ALCOHOL PRESERVES… FOR 40 MILLION YEARS

According to Robert Dudley, a researcher with the University of Austin, natural selection favoured our ripe-fruit-eating ancestors, these fruits being higher in micronutrients and containing one per cent ethanol.

Cocktails
of benefits

With a juicer always at the ready,
plus a well-oiled blender, you'll enjoy
a rainbow of home-made vitamins.

Red berries,
for energy.

FRUITS, VEGETABLES, AND YOUR IMAGINATION
Vitamins are volatile! Drink preparations as soon as they are made to enjoy maximum benefits. Here are some starting ideas to dip into, always in tune with the seasons.

YOUR HEALTH

THE FAVOURITES OF
LAURENCE SALOMON
FOR A HEALTHY GLOW

- carrot
- apple
- fennel

"Fennel provides a fresh note with its aniseed taste."

A TRIO OF MILKS... WITHOUT MILK

- soy milk
- oat milk
- ½ banana
- 1 spoonful of almond or hazelnut butter

... AND FROM THE NUTRITIONIST

- cranberry
- kiwifruit

"Antioxidants are wonderful for cystitis."

ALL SEASONS

SPRING

- strawberries
- orange flower water

SUMMER

- raspberry • apricot
- tomato • celery • coriander

AUTUMN

- grape • lemon • mint

WINTER

- beetroot • apple • kiwifruit
- carrot • coconut • lemon

Add a little zest:
its pretty looks already
do you good.

GOOD SKIN

- pineapple
- milk (or soy milk)
- coconut

PRE-BEACH

- lychee
- kiwifruit
- strawberry

A FEAST FOR THE SUN

- well-ripened mango
- carrot
- plain yoghurt • ginger

A-BOMB

FAVOURITE OF CHEF ROUGUI DIA

- pomegranate juice
- strawberry juice
- redcurrant juice

DETOX

- juice of a lemon
- water (cold in summer, hot in winter)
- a spoonful of honey

RECOVERY

- egg yolk
- almond milk

CRETAN-STYLE

- tomato
- lemon
- cucumber
- basil
- chilli (optional)

OKINAWA-STYLE

- rice milk
- pineapple
- grapefruit
- cinnamon

7

it's in the bag

ON TOP OF MY SHOPPING LIST

Fresh is best

Shopping well is about following the right route: apart from the fresh-food sections of the supermarkets, do your shopping at farmer's markets and small grocery stores, get to know your neighbourhood, buy locally and ethically, and you just might find that it's the new way of being modern!

CHANGES AFOOT IN YOUR SHOPPING BASKET

Our approach to buying food has evolved a great deal. And while the market for ready-made meals hasn't completely swallowed us whole, it's gaining ground. Are we so afraid that it's too complicated to buy (and prepare) fresh food?

Go home-made It's all a matter of organisation. Getting back to the stove and buying seasonal ingredients not only lets you **cook more healthy food, but also save real money**.

SUPER MARKET, FRESH IDEAS

Walk around the stalls, breathe in the perfume of the tomatoes and melons, size up the shine in the eye of a fish or the fine grain of a piece of meat: a source of inspiration that is already part of the pleasure of cooking.

Aim for quality in produce rather than quantity. The waste created by our overweight societies leads to choices that weigh heavily on our energy bill. The fact that the food has more taste and flavour also lets you cook more simply: less fat, less salt, **less fuss. And more benefits**.

BUY IN BUNCHES

More and more common among garden-deprived city-dwellers are market garden operations that let you take advantage of seasonal produce by grouping orders, via the internet or co-op organisations.

Locavore: the ultimate trend

The locavore has arisen as a result of our habit for buying (and demanding) out-of-season produce from the other side of the world, which ramps up our carbon footprint (air transport generates 100 times more CO_2 than sea freight).
A locavore doesn't eat anything that is produced outside a 160km radius of where they live. The only downside: this often means, in principle, going without tea and coffee.
It's not necessary to go to that extreme: choosing locally grown products and ones that respect the environment will still have an impact on our carbon footprint.

Ready-to-eat:
stick to the label

Flush out too-salty, too-fatty, too-sugary foods, unmask additives and other nasties. A few leads to help you find your way through the jungle of the supermarket shelves.

THE LABEL LABYRINTH

How to read the label? Start at the beginning

The order in which the ingredients appear sets the tone: the primary ingredients come first. The later the (bad) fats come, the better for your figure; the same goes for salt. And the longer the list is, the further removed you are from nature.

The real percentages of the ingredients are sometimes well hidden behind the marketing smoke and mirrors. Until new directives for displaying nutritional information come in, vigilance is the rule. There are small books you can slip into your handbag that are a good guide to the additives you need to consume with caution.

THE WORD FROM THE NUTRITIONIST

The **trans-fatty acids** in commercial foods are harmful: they shouldn't represent more than 1 per cent of the lipids we eat. Why are there so many of them? As both a binding agent and flavour enhancer, they hold ingredients together. Fortunately, canola oil is making its appearance. Products subject to overly high temperatures are all problematic.

DUTIFUL CITIZENS

Some distributors display the carbon footprint (the journey the product has undergone and its impact on the environment): a real badge of eco-responsibility.

High price
They're perfect for emergencies, but pre-prepared meals are more expensive and not as healthy as homemade ones.

Hidden salt
Eighty per cent of the salt in our diet comes from processed foods.

SCIENCE NOTE
There are about 3500 artificial flavours that haven't been scientifically studied.

Organic growth

With our new awareness of the importance of our environment as well as our health concerns, organic food no longer has to prove its relevance. Organic food stores have become broader in their appeal, and 'green' aisles are blossoming in most of the large supermarket chains.

BUYING ORGANIC IS ELEMENTARY

Respecting the environment and the earth's produce by minimising the use of pesticides, GMOs (genetically modified organisms) and other chemical additives seems blindingly obvious today. Even if, given the higher production costs, some seem to be luxury items, organic products are becoming more and more accessible and have never been more justified on our plates.

A BETTER NUTRIENT PROFILE

Professor Henri Joyeux has conducted the ABARAC (Organic Agriculture, Sustainable Agriculture, Conventional Agriculture) comparative studies since 2003, which conclude that organic products are superior from a nutritional perspective. What about **animal farming**? Fish fed on food granules with no access to plankton are no longer able to make omega-3. Similarly for cattle, it's the grass they eat that gives the meat its properties: stuffing them with antibiotics and meat-and-bone meal can only raise health questions. And it's a similar story for **fruit and vegetables**, where the overuse of pesticides deprives them of their natural defence mechanisms, and fertilisers disintegrate their fibre. Waterlogged, they are also less flavoursome. **Organic raspberries and strawberries**, for example, offer almost 20 per cent more antioxidant flavonoids than chemically treated fruit, and have more flavour because they are allowed to ripen naturally.

Natural additives, lecithins, pectins and alginates (which have replaced gelatin since the mad cow disease scare) are perfectly permissible in organic-labelled food. On the rare occasions that suspicious traces have been found in biological crops, these have been due to environmental pollution.

Priority vegetables

Carrots, leeks and other salad vegetables, which feed directly on the soil's nitrates (which are converted into nitrites inside the body), are the most affected, so choose organic.

More organic, less aesthetic

Fertilisers produce a uniform, standard-grade product. An organic fruit or vegetable will not present as well: it may have an irregular shape (because it seeks out its nutrients in its own way), its skin may not be smooth, but it has a flavour that's incomparable, and shows the characters of its origin.

THE WORD FROM LAURENCE SALOMON

If you calculate the weight of the ingredients you need to make your own organic biscuits, they are less expensive per kilo than conventional biscuits.

The green aisle:
champion vegetables

It's unanimous: no-one questions their health-giving properties. Do the sums: five serves of vegetables plus two of fruit a day equals health, beauty and happiness.

Fruit or seed, flower or stalk, tuber, sprout or root… the great fruit and vegetable family has something for all tastes. And it's precisely this **variety** that helps them be indispensable, and so healthy.

GOING GREEN: GOOD FOR EVERYONE!

If we're being encouraged to find more reasons to eat our greens, it's ultimately for our own good. The most recent studies only give more support to our parents' claims about broccoli.

Four hundred grams a day: this is the minimum recommended by the WHO as a source of micronutrients (vitamins, mineral salts, trace elements) and antioxidants (beta carotene, vitamins C and E, polyphenols), heralded for their protective benefits against cardiovascular disease, diabetes and some cancers. And best of all, they are filling (thank you, fibre) without leading to weight problems, thanks to their water content. Alternate raw (for maximum vitamins) and cooked, for easier digestion.

CHEESE, FISH OR A FEW VEGIES?

There's **calcium** in spinach, broccoli, cabbage and watercress, **iodine** in leeks and turnips. Vegetables hold up well when compared with traditional sources such as fish and dairy. As for the brain, it's hungry for xanthophyll and lycopene (found in colourful vegies), which **nourish our cognitive functions**.

FROM THE GREEN LEEK TO A BEAN FEAST

Leeks are as low in calories as they are high in carotene, fibre and minerals. And they are available all year round, but it's worth waiting for the arrival of the spring bean crop, light on the calories but not on vitamins C, A, B9, minerals (including calcium and ▶

Lamb's lettuce: an omega-3 lion
A unique phenomenon in the vegetable kingdom, this small lettuce is the king of fatty acids. Dressed with a few walnuts and a drizzle of canola oil, it's a recipe for success

THE WORD FROM THE EXPERT
Beetroot red (betanin, derived from betalain) or carrot orange (carotenoids): our favourite antioxidant foods show their true colours.

magnesium) and fibre. An energising food, beans also gently restore regular bowel movements. Also light, **zucchini** (courgette) are a better choice than their cousins, **eggplants** (aubergine), which can tend to soak up oil a little over-enthusiastically.

TOMATO RED

With its 65 per cent water content and a miniscule 15 calories per 100g, it's our favourite summer fruit. The tomato's antioxidant, **lycopene**, is fully released during cooking and olive oil reinforces its effect. Firm and fleshy with their fragrant stem, garden tomatoes obliterate the memory of the commercial varieties that no longer taste of anything. From the (burst in the mouth) cherry tomatoes to the heirloom varieties being rediscovered (like Black Krim and oxheart), you should eat tomatoes at room temperature for maximum flavour.

C IS FOR CABBAGE (RED, WHITE, GREEN)

It's stuffed full of vitamins C, A and E, low in calories, very filling and a reputed anticarcinogen.

ORANGE (AS IN CARROT)

The pectin and cellulose in carrots do our intestines good (beta carotene isn't their only asset). It's not as high in sugar as its taste would lead us to believe, so its reputation as a beauty food stands firm. As long as you don't overindulge: orange palms will quickly indicate an overdose.

DON'T FORGET THE GARLIC

It contains a good dozen antioxidants all on its own. Or **black radish**, with its essential liver-draining action. Or the **artichoke**, a blessing for the liver. And don't forget the low-calorie **mushroom**. If vegetables don't agree with you completely raw, when their enzyme and vitamin potential is maximised, one solution is **vegetable juices**, since this elminates the indigestible fibre.

LONG LIVE FROZEN VEGIES

Picked and snap-frozen (which avoids damaging the plant cells), they can contain more vitamins than their fresh-bought equivalents, which may have been stored for several days in less than ideal conditions.

Tomato skins recycled as an anti-inflammatory Researchers at the Biomolecular Chemistry Institute in Spain have found a use for the millions of tonnes of waste generated by the manufacture of tomato sauces and pizzas: naturally therapeutic molecules. Science confirms the lessons of experience. The great chef Ghislaine Arabian tells the story: "I rubbed halved tomatoes on my children's sunburn and it worked! They must contain molecules that calm burning."

Capsicum (pepper) skin is hard to digest, which is why you grill them in the oven. Once they blacken, the skin comes off easily.

A soy for all seasons:
luminous legumes

There's no end to the rediscovery of their virtues.
Dried beans and legumes offer a power-packed
alternative to animal protein and gluten.

One flexible chick
The chickpea becomes
hummus in the Middle East,
pakora or *dal* (a turmeric-
spiced purée) in India, *falafel*
in Israel and *panisse* in
Marseille. But it has also
been used to make a very
passable coffee substitute.

Lentils: *dal*-ings
Eaten before a meal,
lentils are an excellent
appetite suppressant.

**THE WORD FROM
THE EXPERT**
The lecithin in soy has
cholesterol-lowering properties
and is also used as an emulsifier
in mayonnaise or chocolate.

MUNG OR TOFU, MILK AND YOGHURT: THE INCREDIBLE PLANET SOY
We love **bean shoots** in stir-fries and salads. But it's a whole other family that gives us **tofu**: a sort of curdled soy milk, sold in compressed cakes and ready to cook. An excellent source of plant protein (twice as much as lentils: 37g per 100g), low in saturated fats and calories, it's ultra-digestible. And it marries well with all sorts of dishes: roasted or grilled, it transforms a vegetable stir-fry. As for **soy milks and yoghurts**, they offer an alternative option from breakfast to afternoon tea. Natural **soy sauces**, such as **tamari**, represent a food in their own right (protein, vitamins, minerals) and an interesting, less salty, alternative to traditional condiments.

QUINOA This South American cousin of spinach and beetroot is bursting with protein and amino acids, magnesium and iron. Highly digestible, it is cooked in the same way as rice.

WHITE BEANS In all their varieties, they are rich sources of iron (without the fat), vitamins E and B6 and calcium. Originally from Mexico, they also exist in red and black varieties.

LENTILS Black (currently being studied for anticarcinogenic properties), **brown**, **green** or **red**, they're ultra-digestible, loaded with phosphorus and folic acid (great for pregnant women), and they have the advantage of cooking quickly and being as exquisite hot as cold.

CHICKPEAS Generously endowed with selenium, potassium, zinc and manganese, as well as being a diuretic and antioxidant, chickpeas also eliminate urea.

Healthy sprouts:
shooting stars

Germination, the key moment when the tiny seed concentrates all its powers on becoming a real plant, unleashes such energy that its vitamins, minerals and trace elements are multiplied to an incredible extent.

TINY VITAMIN BOMBS

The success of the sprout (which has spread beyond the health food sphere to the tables of fashionable restaurants) is not just because of their deliciously acidic flavour, freshness and crisp texture which adds a touch of originality to salads, sandwiches and other meat and fish dishes; it is also because their properties are unique in the sense that a sprout offers **3–12 times more nutrients** than the grain or mature plant, including enzymes and rare essential fatty acids.

As for **vitamins,** they make spectacular leaps:

• vitamin B6: more than 200 per cent

• vitamins A and B2: more than 300 per cent

• vitamin C: more than 600 per cent

What can top that?

MUNCH THEM RAW

The shoots of plants such as quinoa, alfalfa or radishes; legumes such as edamame (soy beans), lentils, and oil seeds (sesame, linseed); grains such as buckwheat, rice, barley (and even wheat), all rival each other in their virtues and taste, to be mixed and matched as you like.

Sprouting at home
Fresher and less expensive than the ready-to-eat punnets, seeds can be sprouted in a germinator or simply in containers covered with a tea towel. It's not difficult but is a bit finicky because you need to rinse them each morning and evening until the sprout appears. Sprouts have a short lifespan (they stop at 5cm), so make sure you always have some by staggering your 'plantings'.

THE WORD FROM THE EXPERT
Eat sprouts for breakfast; such an influx of vitamins will get you going.

Fruits: a sweet passion

The garden of earthly delights has long tempted us with edible flowering plants. The good news is that there's no need to resist the jewel of so many healthy, sweet dishes.

Two to three serves of fruit a day is ideal. One serve is...
- 1 raw or cooked apple, unsweetened
- 1 pear
- 1 orange
- ½ grapefruit
- 2 mandarins
- 150g (2 slices) fresh pineapple
- 150g kiwifruit (2)
- 100g cherries (about 20)
- 150g strawberries (1 cup)
- 1 peach
- 4 fresh figs
- 1 nectarine
- 3 very large apricots (or 5 small)
- 2 plums (or 3 small)
- 80g grapes (a small bunch)
- 80g banana (1 small)
- 150g unsweetened fruit compote
- 150g unsweetened fruit salad in natural juice.

THE FRUIT OF LONG RESEARCH

In 1989, at the annual medical conference the Bichat discussions, Dr Andrée Giraud demonstrated a spectacular drop in cholesterol by giving her patients three apples a day without changing their diet.

THE GRAPE

Three cheers to grapes for their flavonoids and polyphenols, including the now-famous **resveratrol** (also found in **raspberries, blackberries** and **bilberries**), for their anti-ageing functions, their anti-osteoporotic qualities, and their role as a heart-protection shield. The grape improves the metabolism of fats, weighs in at 72 calories per 100g (due to its fructose content), and has plenty of potassium or vitamin C, B and niacin. These nutrients tend to be concentrated in **the skin and the seeds**. A short grape 'cure' (two days maximum), for which organic grapes are a must as they are especially sensitive to pesticides, can let the system gently cleanse itself after a period of overindulgence.

THE BIG-HEARTED FIG

A heavyweight anti-cholesterol agent, the fig is also good for the heart thanks to its **anthocyanins**, and polyphenols that are robust enough to strengthen the veins and prevent the formation of artery-clogging fat. Cherries, grapes, bilberries, blackberries and blackcurrants also enjoy these properties.

PEAR: THE THIRST-QUENCHER

An excellent diuretic, the pear is also a first-class thirst quencher. Like the **peach**, the pear's gentle fibre and anti-bloating content works against water retention.

▶

► THE APPLE OF YOUR EYE

Ever since Eve, this fruit has stood apart from the rest: 'An apple a day keeps the doctor away' is a piece of wisdom that is even found in Chinese medicine. Fibre, vitamins by the bucketful and ultra-digestible pectins make it a real blessing for the digestive system.

LEMON

A real delight: apart from its antioxidant and immunity-stimulating vitamin C content, its **limoneme** acts as an excellent antiseptic. Lemons fragrant zest lifts the flavour of other fruit; add it to compotes (organic lemons only), and use its juice in fruit salads to replace sugar as a flavour enhancer.

ORANGE, AS IN APRICOT...

With a generous dose of beta carotene (a precursor to vitamin A), iron and copper, and fibre, apricots have everything you need to keep your skin beautiful. And great for avoiding cramps thanks to the potassium.

... OR ROCKMELON

With a heady perfume, these melons also offer vitamin B9, folic acid (good for future mums), potassium and carotene.

RED LIKE A STRAWBERRY...

The darling bud of summer, strawberries are dosed up with vitamin C and 90 per cent water.

... OR A MALTESE ORANGE

A delicate balance between tart and sweet, the most generous of the juicing oranges brings sunshine into winter.

GO BANANAS

Blessed with a mood-elevating and stabilising hormone, anti-fatigue qualities and an incredible wealth of nutrients, the banana is a reliable standby for breakfast or afternoon snack.

FRESH... BUT FOR HOW LONG?

Vitamin levels in fruit drop quickly. Given that picking them from our own orchard is impossible for most of us, we should shop a few times a week and not put fruit in the fridge (it destroys their flavour). As for organic fruits, they're a true fleeting pleasure: you'll recognise their authenticity through their lack of preservatives. As with vegetables, frozen fruits can fill in the gaps, especially out of season.

Pomegranate: a nutrient bomb
Researchers have recently discovered how potent the 'thousand seeds' of the pomegranate are. Pomegranate juice helps blood circulation —it's a vein stimulant that eliminates bad cholesterol by making the arteries more supple and protecting them against cardiovascular disease. You can drink a glass when you wake up in the morning, straight or diluted with water.

THE WORD FROM THE EXPERT
KIWI: OUI OUI!
Known for its record-level vitamin C content, it continues to ripen after being picked. Its only downside is that it can cause allergies.

Meat: give it the chop?

The flagship source of protein, which builds muscle mass.
Meat is a matter of quality rather than quantity.

Guinea fowl: a Guinness record for health
It has no more calories than white fish (such as cod).

Long live the organic chicken
An organic chicken is entitled to a minimum lifespan of 90 days (compared to 42 days for a battery chicken) to develop and roam freely. The result is less fat, more protein and flesh that responds better to cooking. And organic animal rearing generates 30 per cent less carbon dioxide.

THE WORD FROM THE EXPERT
It takes 10–15kg grain to produce 1kg beef; 5 kg to produce 1kg pork; and 4kg to produce 1kg chicken. A report from the Food and Agriculture Organisation of the United Nations calculated that by eating one steak less per week, we could save enough grain to feed the planet.

CARNE DIEM!

The virtues of meat are undeniable, thanks in particular to its **vitamins, iron** and **amino acids**. The latter improve mood and sleep, and guard against fatigue as well. But meat is also a source of saturated fats and toxins (connected to the stress of industrial animal farming). So without depriving ourselves of gastronomic marvels, like a tender *pot au feu* or sweet little lamb chops, the **trend** is towards eating meat less often, but of a higher quality. Aim for eating meat no more than three to four times per week, in serving sizes of 120–150g, preferably **lean**, and paired with vegetables.

THE CHOICE CUTS?

Red meat Sirloin, eye fillet, hanger steak, skirt steak, rump steak and duck breast (without its fat it has less calories than a beef fillet).

White Guinea fowl, chicken (skinless), turkey, pork tenderloin, and veal escalope.

GET TO KNOW YOUR BUTCHER

The meat industry offers all kinds of options, at all price levels. Now that meat origins are more traceable, it's easier to get information: from industrial meat producers to top-level organic farming (where the animals are antibiotic-free and graze on pesticide-free grass); from the pre-packaged items sold under plastic to the artisan butcher, there's a wide variety of possibilities. The organic option, again, is the best avenue by far.

... AND YOUR SAUSAGE MAKER

Try eating organic, free-range pork. *Boudin noir* (blood sausage—which has the most iron of all foods, and the iron is more easily absorbed than the iron in spinach), ham and prosciutto are all sources of vitamin B. The good news is that, in Okinawa, pork is the official pro-longevity meat. As long as you like the head and trotters.

The school of fish:
scaling great heights

Generally acclaimed by nutritionists, and highly recommended as an alternative to meat for carnivores, the fruits of the sea are riding the crest of a health wave.

FISH SCHOOL

Studies confirm the protective function of fish against cardiovascular disease (and anti-ageing and blood-thinning benefits): it's no surprise that longer-living populations eat large amounts of fish. Their polyunsaturated fatty acids (omega-3s) are a hot topic in nutritional research. Eat **lean** or **oily fish**—eel, herring, salmon, trout, tuna, anchovy, pilchard, sardine—two or three times a week. Ask the fishmonger to leave the skin on (to retain the protective fat between the skin and the flesh), unless you are planning to eat the fish raw. If eating fish raw, buy it ultra-fresh and always freeze it beforehand (freezing eliminates any parasites that may be present).

THE WORD FROM NUTRITIONIST DR ARNAUD COCAUL

Farmed fish should be enriched with **phytoplankton** one month before being sold at market, otherwise their omega-3 levels won't be high enough, and their nutritional benefit won't be the same. As for wild-caught fish, these can, on the other hand, contain concentrations of heavy metals. Shark, bluefin tuna and other high-sea fish shouldn't be eaten by pregnant women. Instead choose **big-eye, yellowfin or albacore tuna**.

SEAFOODS: AN ODE TO IODINE AND ZINC

Fish represent an incredible concentration of nutritional delights for very few calories: fish equals a health feast that boosts our immune system. And add a short **seaweed** cure to finish on a high note; you should eat at least 10g every day.

The freshness advantage
Forget the sayings about buying oysters in months with or without an 'r'; they're good all year round.

Prawn fishing: the net cost
It's better to choose prawns from quality farmers than wild-caught prawns, where overfishing is doing a lot of damage.

Eggs:
all in the same basket?

Poached or in an omelette, fried or boiled, in a sauce, a mousse or a cake, sweet or savoury… eggs are a nutritional wonder. There's more than one reason to bring them out of their shell.

ON A (GOOD CHOLESTEROL) HIGH

It's true that there's cholesterol in egg yolk, but this is completely absorbed due to its lecithin. A good reason to vote for an egg a day is apart from its lipids, it's a nutritional delight, high in proteins, phosphorus, iron, zinc and vitamins A, D and E.

A HARD-BOILED CASE

There's no question: if we're talking about raw egg (present in dishes from chocolate mousse to homemade mayonnaise) or soft-boiled eggs, buying free-range eggs or organic ones is the best option. They are the most protected against bacteria, such as salmonella. Another requirement: buy **extra fresh** every time. Fried, scrambled or in an omelette, it's how they're cooked that gives eggs their personality. It also ranks them on a scale from the healthier (boiled or poached) to the less digestible (scrambled in butter) options.

THE DIETITIAN'S TIP

Eat two hard-boiled eggs before leaving for a cocktail party (or any place where you'll be exposed to temptation): it's the best weapon against cravings.

Don't wash the egg shell
This removes its protective coating. Keep eggs at room temperature or in the door of the refrigerator, the warmest part of the fridge. For soft-boiled eggs, ideally use eggs within five days of being laid. After that, they're still good to eat in cooked forms.

THE WORD FROM THE EXPERT
Why buy eggs enriched with omega-3s? Because chickens no longer get to forage for the greenery and slugs that are natural sources of fatty acids.

Two eggs equals:
- 150 calories
- 13g protein
- 11g lipids
- 0.13g sodium.

As good as fresh bread

Starches, beginning with bread, no longer have a bad reputation: on the contrary, they play a perfect part in any balanced diet...

STARCHES... THE COMEBACK KIDS!

Their good qualities are gathering momentum, with nutritional studies backing low-GI carbs in particular. By encouraging the production of serotonin, 'slow' sugars (or complex carbohydrates) are as effective as their faster cousins when it comes to **making us happy**. But on top of that, rather than making us fat, they fuel our muscles, minimise the stockpiling of fats, help keep us regular, fill us up so we avoid the cravings that lead to compulsive eating and have a calming effect, encouraging a peaceful night's sleep. So, it's a good idea to invite your favourite grains to dinner. The daily dose (250g cooked weight) can be divided up according to taste. For example, 30g of uncooked rice or pasta has a cooked weight of 100g.

MULTIPLYING OF THE LOAVES

From artisan to mass-produced products, the **vogue for novel kinds of bread** multiplies the choices at the bakery. Bring on the **wholemeal breads** (especially **sourdough** which ferments the flour and cancels out the negative effects of gluten by 'predigesting' it) and those using organic flours; they're better choices than white bread, which makes you feel stuffed without being satisfied and has high-GI carbohydrates that are immediately released into the blood. As with all foods, chew your bread well, so that the enzymes in the saliva can start off the digestive process and prevent bloating.

Grains: the whole(meal) package
Combined with pulses, they are a delicious source of plant protein.

Need your morning toast?
Alternatives for those intolerant of wheat gluten are buckwheat (as light crispbreads) and rice (as rice cakes).

Potatomania:
a vegetable for all seasons

*With their reputation restored, potatoes deserve to be rediscovered…
And, as they come in all shapes, sizes and colours,
there's something for everyone!*

An incredible palette
Which even includes
the striking purple-fleshed
vitelotte potato.

THE WORD FROM
THE DIETITIAN
Fries and mashed potatoes have
the highest glycaemic index. Don't
overindulge: Walter Willet, Head of
Harvard's School of Public Health,
recommends limiting consumption
because their high starch levels
don't suit our sedentary lifestyle.
Combining potatoes with other
vegetables makes them easier to
digest by further lowering their
glycaemic index.

NEW SEASON POTATOES: ENJOY SKINS AND ALL

Harvested before they're fully grown, the small new potatoes,
light and with a high water content, are a feast to enjoy in their
skins (so thin it scrapes off easily), steamed or in a salad. But they
don't suit mash (their starch hasn't developed yet) or chips. Full
of sugars and vitamins (four times as much as their bigger
siblings), this nourishing marvel, won't even make you put on
weight when served plain. A health tip: simply cut them in half
lengthways and put them on the oven rack, with nothing added;
they naturally puff up and give off a wonderful aroma. Enjoy them
golden brown, just as they are, with butter, or a drizzle of olive oil.

FOR STORING

While new potatoes are eaten very fresh (especially organic ones,
and those that haven't undergone 'ionising' treatments), other
potatoes, harvested when mature, keep all year round. From kipfler
potatoes or the tiny grenaille or charlotte to the larger varieties
(bintje, desiree, spunta) and the more floury potatoes, this is a
versatile vegetable: whether you prefer them as a mash or purée,
as a gratin or as chips, potatoes can handle it all.

Bon état général
Prix:1 000 €

Pasta: use your noodle

Italian pasta or Chinese noodles, they've conquered the whole world. The very model of a complete meal, they come in all shapes, and are made from a wide variety of ingredients.

HARD OR SOFT WHEAT, WHITE OR WHOLEMEAL

With almost no fat, and lots of carbohydrates, pasta is especially good at satisfying our appetite. But their nutritional qualities vary a great deal between white pastas (low fibre) and wholemeal pastas (which provide 20 per cent of your daily fibre in one serving.)

IN GOOD COMPANY

Unless they're drowning in an overly rich sauce, pasta and noodles present no health problem at all. They contain plant protein, minerals, starch and complex carbohydrates that work against impulse binges; with their sugars released slowly into the body, they're the favourite energy source of athletes. Made with or without eggs, it's the same story: 180 calories per 200g cooked noodles.

PASS THE PASTA

Make sure you don't overdo the cream, butter and cheese (parmesan has the advantage of being one of the tastier cheeses, so you naturally use less). As for other sauces, pasta combines well with the lycopenes and other antioxidants in our favourite vegetables, with tomatoes at the top of the list. Wonderful in salads (with olive oil and fresh herbs), pasta and noodles are also useful additions to soup (from exquisite Italian minestrones to Chinese rice vermicelli soups). As for homemade fresh pasta, see Nadia Santini's stuffed ravioli (recipe page 190).

It's the dose that matters
Stick to 50g uncooked weight per person.

Stock in trade
Cooking pasta and noodles in a fragrant stock will allow you to reduce the amount of salt you add to the water and sauce.

Secret sauce
What's the key to a perfect marriage between pasta and sauce? Heat the sauce (bought or homemade, or even a mixture of the two) in a large frying pan and add the cooked pasta two minutes before the end of the cooking time. It will soak up the sauce and arrive at the table piping hot.

Rice:
the land of the gluten-free

A kernel of genius, and still the staple food of half the planet, rice keeps reinventing itself, showing off its countless virtues.

EVERYONE'S FAVOURITE

According to the Japanese, a meal without rice is not a meal. And they'd get no argument from China: rice and food are synonymous there. If rice is a universally tolerated food (it contains no gluten), it's because it has the special quality of not having mutated genetically for the past ten thousand years. Since 2005, its genome has even been 95 per cent decoded.

THE UNABRIDGED VERSION...

Antioxidant, anti-cholesterol, anti-ageing, and filling, rice is also recommended for its ability to calm intestinal upsets. **Brown or wholemeal rice**, is high in starch; offers magnesium, fibre, selenium and manganese, all excellent active ingredients wrapped up in its package (only its inedible husk has been removed); and it retains all of its fibre and nutrients, unlike white rice. The parboiled version of the latter (where the nutrients are driven into the grain) is better than the precooked varieties, where the substance of the rice is eliminated to make it quick to cook. Basmati, the most fragrant rice (it contains 12 times more odour molecules than its colleagues) is also the least sugary of the white rice varieties.

THE RICE BOWL

As a pilaf, cooked in a saffron-scented broth, enlivened with spices, turmeric or poppy seeds, hot or as a salad, rice goes just as well with vegetables as it does with meat and fish. And it loves all sauces. **It's the dose that matters:** 50g uncooked rice per person.

Puffed rice cakes

These are handy and healthy (although high-GI). Choose organic or brown rice versions as an alternative to corn bread.

The rice rainbow

Italian round-grained (arborio rice–long live risotto), Indian basmati rice for biryanis, Thai glutinous rice, Camargue rice... Fair trade organisations are introducing us to wholegrain rices from Vietnam that are red, black, purple, pink and green, full of vitamins with an irresistible *al dente* texture. As for 'wild' rice, it's a rice in name only: it is actually an American grass seed.

Milk, butter, cheese:
dairy queens

They are no longer considered to be the only source of calcium, but they make a delicious contribution to a balanced diet.

Think you're too old to drink milk? Wrong! Fermented dairy products are much more digestible than normal milk, as long as you choose them well.

KEEPING IT NATURAL: RAW, FARMHOUSE, ORGANIC

Look for good farmhouse or organic cheeses (made from raw milk, if possible) whose lactose is completely transformed in the fermentation process and whose protein is more easily absorbed. According to naturopath and chef Laurence Salomon, listeria might even be more likely to grow in pasteurised milk than raw milk, which is protected by saprophytic micro-organisms. The **casein** in goat's milk cheese (the cheese that's lowest in fat) and sheep's milk cheese is also more easily absorbed than that in cow's milk.

COCKTAIL HOUR

Cheese and crudités: a delicious and substantial accompaniment to drinks, and a great way to remind yourself of the marriage made in heaven between cheese, fruit and vegetables. Remember: the harder the cheese, the higher it is in calcium, but also in **saturated fats**.

THE WORD FROM THE NUTRITIONIST, DR ARNAUD COCAUL

Say yes to dairy products, but **not with every meal**. It's best to avoid eating meat and cheese in the same meal, to avoid excess saturated fats. And always keep a good acid-alkaline balance in mind: feel free to have some *tartiflette*, as long as you only have a fruit salad for dessert!

The lowdown
Yoghurts are not high in fat, unless they contain added cream. Flavoured milk drinks or ones mixed with fruit are high in sugar (the equivalent of at least two teaspoons of sugar per drink) and some are very high in fat. Check the percentage of lipids before giving in to temptation.

Essential oils

All hail the good oil.
Vegetable oils complete the nutritional palette
by offering us the fruits of their flavours.
Use them to cook with or to dress salads.

FATTY ACIDS: OUTLOOK NOT SO SUNNY FOR SUNFLOWER OIL!

CANOLA OIL (containing both omega-3s and 9s) is the only oil to have proved itself when it comes to cardiovascular protection. It shares a particular biochemical trait with fish (and linseed oil): its polyunsaturated fatty acids help to lower triglycerides, therefore preventing cardiovascular illness. It tolerates heat (to 160°C), but loses some of its properties when heated and gives off a smell that's reminiscent of fish.

OLIVE OIL contains monounsaturated fatty acids that offer protection against cardiovascular disease when combined with a Mediterranean-style diet and make it an excellent food for lowering cholesterol. Not to mention a gastronomic delight.

The ideal is **extra-virgin cold-pressed oil**, as little refined as possible, from small and organic producers. More or less fruity, the different *terroirs* enhance the oil's qualities, just like varieties of wine.

TWO OILS ARE BETTER THAN ONE

FOR COOKING USE olive and peanut oil.

Develop a light touch; a good habit is to use a brush to spread a thin coat on the base of the frying pan.

FOR SALADS USE canola and olive (blends are good), but also walnut, hazelnut, linseed, sesame, argan and grapeseed. The more aromatic the oil, the less you will need.

What's in a label?

The agrifood industry and producers use a great deal of sunflower, corn, grapeseed and palm oil in their packaged products. One more reason to avoid using them at home!

THE WORD FROM THE NUTRITIONIST
GOOD CHOLESTEROL

Like most of the substances our body secretes, cholesterol is essential to our body's system. So, a lack of cholesterol (hypocholesterolemia) leads to negative effects. On the other hand, having excess cholesterol (hypercholesterolemia), can indicate problems, yet is not always a risk factor for cardiovascular disease. It's more complex than what the media reports—your health professional can help you with this.

Salt and sugar:
my best enemies?

They are an integral part of our culinary history. Often put in the sin bin, it is excess that is the real problem. Moderation is key!

ON THE SWEET SIDE: SACCHAROSE

White, raw and brown sugar don't contain any vitamins or minerals. They are empty calories, but very versatile as a condiment or ingredient. They can be added to dairy products, cereals, and fruit, which are themselves sources of vitamins and minerals.

Whether it comes from cane or beets, sugar is 99.9 per cent saccharose (all plants with chlorophyll contain sugar), in which two molecules, fructose and glucose, fight it out for top billing.

A GOOD RAP

Brown, organic, unrefined cane sugar, such as *rapadura*, have a powerful flavour which means you can use less.

THE SALT SCOURGE

INSERM (French National Institute for Health and Medical Research) researcher Pierre Meneton accused salt of being a killer… and the simple verdict is that he's right. It's been established that excess salt causes hypertension, the second leading risk factor for stroke in developed countries. We know that processed food is the main source of salt, so check the label for both sodium and salt content (to work it out, multiply sodium by 2.5).

IT'S ORGANIC

Grey sea salt, brimming with trace elements, is also more aromatic and flavourful than regular table salt.

Salt: another way round

Is potassium salt better than sodium chloride? It's a good idea to wean your tastebuds off salty flavours in general and get your potassium fix in fruits and vegetables.

Sweeteners: false economy

Synthetic sugars scramble the satisfaction messages: the brain waits for the sugar to know that it's satisfied. But sugar substitutes aren't able to send the signal. Therefore, there's a tendency to keep eating.

THE WORD FROM THE EXPERT

Weaning yourself off sugar in tea and coffee? It's simply a matter of educating your tastes: once you've dropped the habit, you pull just as much of a face when drinking a sweetened coffee as when you first tasted its bitterness. Lower the amount of sugar in your baking by flavouring with cinnamon, orange flower water and other spices. And not putting the salt shaker on the table is the best way to forget to add (too much) salt.

Smart spices

An excellent weapon against too much salt or sugar, spices reveal and enhance flavours, and shower us with benefits. From turmeric to cinnamon via pepper and vanilla, take a tour of the spice world with Bruno Jarry, an enlightened Parisian spice merchant.

JADED FROM FLAVOUR ENHANCERS

Bring on the spices to give you back your taste for life! They smooth and bring out flavours without masking them. They're added to enhance a dish without impingeing on its personality. **They're a solution to every health-beauty issue:** you can reduce salt, sugar and fat all the while providing (yourself) pleasure, giving off aromas that stimulate the appetite and help with digestion, among other numerous preventative virtues.

CINNAMON

This dessert fairy is perfect for reducing the amount of sugar in cakes and other desserts, in addition to being valuable for its antiseptic and stimulating properties. Baked apples with cinnamon don't need butter and hardly any sugar. The same goes for exquisite **vanilla**, which is an excellent tonic.

TURMERIC AND PEPPER ARE A ROYAL MARRIAGE

Both anti-inflammatory and antioxidant, and excellent for good circulation, **curcumin** (the active chemical in turmeric) sweeps the prize pool in its health benefits. A cousin of the miraculous **ginger** (an aphrodisiac that is also good for digestion), turmeric ranks highly in the popularity stakes in Okinawa. And combining it with **pepper** (which helps to digest fats and sugars) boosts our ability to absorb its antioxidants.

CHILLI, NO FEAR

Wilbur Scoville rated chillies from 1 to 10 (based on how much it needed to be diluted to soften its heat), from the habanero (10) to the bird's eye (7) to the capsicum (pepper, 0). Antispasmodic and antiseptic, chilli is, paradoxically, good for the stomach.

THE WORD FROM THE EXPERT

It's often thought that, in the Middle Ages, spices were used in a heavy-handed way to neutralise the taste of gamey meat or rotting fish. Not true: fish arrived at market as fresh as today's fish in Paris, it was simply a matter of flaunting wealth, because spices were very expensive! The lower classes, for their part, made do with herbs.

THE PIONEER OF VITAMIN C

It was a Hungarian scientist who first isolated vitamin C, in paprika. A good reason to add a little of this peppery spice to your life.

►

▶ **THE REST...**

Cloves are renowned for their antiseptic properties: an onion studded with a clove can redeem a *pot au feu* if the meat isn't tip-top. **Cardamom** and **caraway** have digestive properties; **cumin** is good for bloating and calms the appetite.

The **tonka bean** started its career in the perfume industry and today many chefs are using it in very small quantities. It tastes like **nutmeg** and is a hallucinogen (in very large doses). No risk with the refreshing and crunchy **blue poppy seeds**, widely used in Eastern European baking and exquisite in vegetable dishes: it's the resin of the poppy that is the source of opium. **Raz al hanout** is not just good for tagines: this cocktail of 20 spices transforms vegetables or rice.

ADD SPICE...

Sprinkle over at the end of cooking or grind directly over the dish: the ideal conditions for developing the aromas.

FROM A TASTE FOR ADVENTURE TO ADVENTURES OF TASTE

The travels of spice-merchant Bruno Jarry have taken him to all corners of the world: India, for example, where he works in partnership on sustainable development projects with spice producers in Kerala, a verdant southern state. He offers support to 1500 farmers who, in the 1990s, launched themselves into the organic production of rare peppers, which stimulate the culinary imagination: green, white, and black, their effect is unbeatable.

"I'm happy just observing the effects of spices on my customers," says Bruno. "I don't present myself as a substitute for a doctor. But it's true there was a Lorient pharmacist, Mr Gosse, who perfected a fabulous curry mix that he sold in his dispensary."

THE WORD FROM THE SPICE MERCHANT

It's better to buy spices whole rather than ground (apart from turmeric, which is too hard), and in small quantities (their shelf life is a maximum of six months to one year). Store them away from humidity, light and air to keep their flavour intact, in a drawer or metal box. Only sesame and poppy seeds (with a higher oil content) should be kept in the refrigerator.

GRIND YOUR OWN

You can use a small coffee grinder to make your own spice mixtures (pulse soft bread to remove the aromas between grinds). A mill with a ceramic mechanism is preferable to a stainless steel one, which is perfect for pepper but less suited to other spices.

Dried fruit and nuts:
fuel up

Lots of calories in a small package, dried fruit and nuts are the ideal snack for energy slumps. Precious allies, they're better than chocolate for raising the bar.

FRUITS AND SEEDS: SUPER FUEL

Dried fruit, by losing up to 90 per cent of its water content, multiplies its energy density by six. It is a rich source of vitamins (with the sole exception of vitamin C, which prefers fresh foods), fibre and minerals. **Prunes**, gentle laxatives, are powerful antioxidants, and are supposed to be as effective against bone-density loss as for keeping a youthful mind. **Raisins, grapes and sultanas** (B2, excellent for the skin and mucous membranes), **dates** (iron and fibre, a wonderful energy booster), **apricots** (laxative and calming) and **figs** (whose fibre helps with regularity) have so many health-giving qualities.

WALNUTS, HAZELNUTS, PISTACHIOS, ALMONDS...

Nuts belong to a misunderstood food group due to our obsession with thinness: the irony is that their (good) cholesterol helps with weight-loss. On top of that, their **essential fatty acids** protect the vascular system and help the nervous system function well. **Pistachios** contain protein and vitamins to strengthen our defences, **hazelnuts** contain protein and vitamin B2 and **walnuts**, whose resemblance to little brains is no accident, are valuable thanks to their phosphorus and magnesium. Naturopath and chef Laurence Salomon recommends eating a couple of walnuts a day as an appetite suppressant.

IT'S ORGANIC

With all of these products, choose organic—although more expensive, you'll be getting a higher quality product meaning that you can eat them in smaller quantities.

Fruitful Venture

Just like fresh fruit, it's best to wash dried fruit before eating it. Pay attention to its colour: if your dried apricots are bright orange it's because of additives (sulphur dioxide). As for dates, if they're shiny, it's because they're glazed with glucose syrup.

Almonds: back in the good books

Recently exonerated by a study in the *British Journal of Nutrition*, the delicious almond is a perfect appetite suppressant. Its undeniably high calorie content is compensated by its ability to satisfy. Conclusion: you eat less of other things.

Happiness therapy:
honey and natural syrups

Honey: gift of nature and thing of wonder. Calming or stimulating, healing and immunity-boosting—thank you, bees. Agave and maple syrup also sweeten the deal.

130 TIMES SWEETER THAN SUGAR.

Honey has up to 80 per cent sugar, but much fewer calories than sugar. The explanation? It contains very little saccharose: the runnier it is, the higher it is in **fructose**; **glucose** makes it crystallise. On top of that, it's 20 per cent water, with mineral salts, trace elements and vitamins (especially B). For best health benefits look for organically produced honey. It is best when extracted at a temperature lower than 42°C and produced by bees who haven't been made to eat sugar.

A **spoonful of honey in tea** is a delicious remedy for a sore throat and helps to digest the bread or toast it is spread on.

Honey from chestnut pollen is especially spectacular: eaten mixed with fruit, it delivers high levels of selenium, making it a formidable weapon against physical and mental fatigue. **Propolis** is a natural antiseptic, used for sore throats and digestive problems.

As for **royal jelly**, the true caviar of the plant world with its anti-ageing and anti-stress properties, its pantothenic acid (vitamin B5) makes it an incredible immune system booster. As a spring cure (mix with honey to soften the bitter taste), you're guaranteed vitality and an elevated mood. Honey was **Hippocrates** favourite medicine.

AGAVE SYRUP This traditional sweet Aztec nectar is derived from the cactus. It has a high sweetening power and low glycaemic index.

Maple syrup: the other natural wonder

The sap flows from a cut made right into the tree trunk. Maple syrup contains sacchorose, but also an admirable set of minerals (manganese, riboflavin and zinc) that are almost non-existent in honey and brown sugar, and totally absent from white sugar. As a bonus, it's full of phenolic compounds and flavonoids, and goes through a completely natural process of evaporation (which means zero additives). The Quebec-based chef Diane Tremblay (*Le Privilege*) makes good use of its unique flavour, which works wonders not only on crêpes, yoghurt and other desserts but also in marinades and hot or cold sauces.

Chocolate: fair and square?

Chocolate is the most delectable antidepressant available over the counter. Its effects are felt far and wide: it's found in all kinds of recipes and even heralded for its cosmetic properties.

DARK PLEASURE

Mood-lifting chocolate, with its serotonin, potassium, magnesium and **antioxidants**, is indulgence without the guilt. Another good piece of news: half a block of chocolate contains **less calories than a croissant**. Two large squares a day is the dose recommended by nutritionists. Don't forget, of course, that it still contains saturated fat.

Breathing in the aroma of cocoa is supposed to be a powerful antidote to low moods. And the smell of a chocolate cake in the oven immediately wakes up the taste buds and evokes the memories of childhood.

THE WORD FROM THE EXPERT
In 2003, in the journal *Nature*, Italian scientists demonstrated that dark chocolate (not milk chocolate) was excellent for circulation.

Aztec Gold
The Aztec emperors drank chocolate flavoured with vanilla and chilli.

Good for mums to be
A study published in the journal *Epidemiology* claims that eating dark chocolate every day during pregnancy reduces the risk of pre-eclampsia by 69 per cent.

ME, DEPRIVED? NEVER! THE WORD FROM NATURAPATH AND CHEF LAURENCE SALOMON

Depriving ourselves upsets the balance of our psychological relationship with food and drives us to the opposite extreme, overcompensating. A typical situation: in a restaurant, you deny yourself the chocolate cake you see on the menu because it's 'banned' on your diet. The craving grows stronger but you block it, choosing the fruit salad instead, only to later leap on a whole block of chocolate. You still end up eating chocolate but at a time when maybe your body isn't able to absorb it as well as it could have during the meal, when the chocolate sugars and fats would have been balanced by other food groups.

8

action!

ON TOP OF THE STOVE

Chain reaction:
freshen up your approach

Consistent hygiene and an impeccable 'cold chain' in handling food are two essential conditions for protecting yourself against the risk of food poisoning.

KEEP IT ON ICE

Cold is the best weapon able to slow down the proliferation of the micro-organisms (such as salmonella) found in fresh food. As long as you don't break the chain. The essential formula: **a fridge kept at the right temperature** and thoroughly cleaned once a month. While it's absolutely essential for meats to be wrapped and chilled (the number of microbes in a hamburger at room temperature doubles every 20 minutes), most vegetables can survive two or three days outside the refrigerator (but beetroot, lettuce and brussels sprouts should be washed and kept inside the fridge). Whether wrapped or naked, items shouldn't touch each other.

Don't keep food past the use-by dates. Homemade sauces (such as mayonnaise and mousse) and cooked meats only get a day's grace, and don't keep leftovers for more than two.

Choose frozen foods last when you're shopping and put them inside a cooler bag. And **always thaw foods in the refrigerator**, never at room temperature, to avoid the proliferation of microbes.

A guide of where to store chilled foods:
- **Vegetable crisper: 6°C**
Washed fruits and vegetables, packaged cheeses.
- **Middle: 0–4°C**
Meats, delicatessen products and fresh fish, cheeses, fresh juice, homemade dishes.
- **Top: 4–6°C**
Dairy products, cooked dishes and meats, ripe cheeses.
- **Door: 6–10°C**
Eggs, butter, milk, drinks.
- **Freezer: -18°C**
Ice cream and frozen foods (discard if the packaging has frosted up).

THE WORD FROM THE EXPERT

Don't confuse 'best before' and 'use-by' dates: throw the item away when the latter is passed (apart from yoghurts).

Peeling and washing:
essential basics

*The sign of a good chef is a well-kept kitchen,
especially since hygiene and healthy
food are excellent housemates.*

WASHING YOUR HANDS

It should be automatic before handling food. Wash for at least 30 seconds with soap and warm water.

PRECIOUS SKIN

Vegetable and fruit skin is the refuge of vitamins, fibre and minerals, but also traces of pesticide and other post-harvest treatments. **Rinse well** under running water. There are five times more vitamins in the skin of an apple than in the rest of the fruit, unlike the pear.

Soaking drowns minerals, so immerse non-organic fruits and vegetables in vinegared water for just a few seconds to remove fertiliser and pesticides.

BENCHMARK PLANS

Wooden bench tops and cutting boards are less hygienic than materials such as plastic, but so much more appealing. To clean them, sprinkle with table salt and some lemon juice (with a drop of essential lemon oil, if possible), rub using a cut lemon and rinse in hot water. Let them air dry.

**THE WORD FROM
THE NATUROPATH**
A vegetable scrubber made from coconut fibres (rot-proof), imported from Japan, is available in many organic stores. It lets you scrub fruits and vegetables whose skin you want to protect (apples, some soft-skinned pears, radishes, turnips, zucchini (courgettes) and new potatoes. You brush while rinsing under the tap at the same time. It's ideal for organic apple compotes: brushing them means they're well-washed, yet you still keep the skin and the core, which holds the precious pectin that gives the compote its lovely texture.

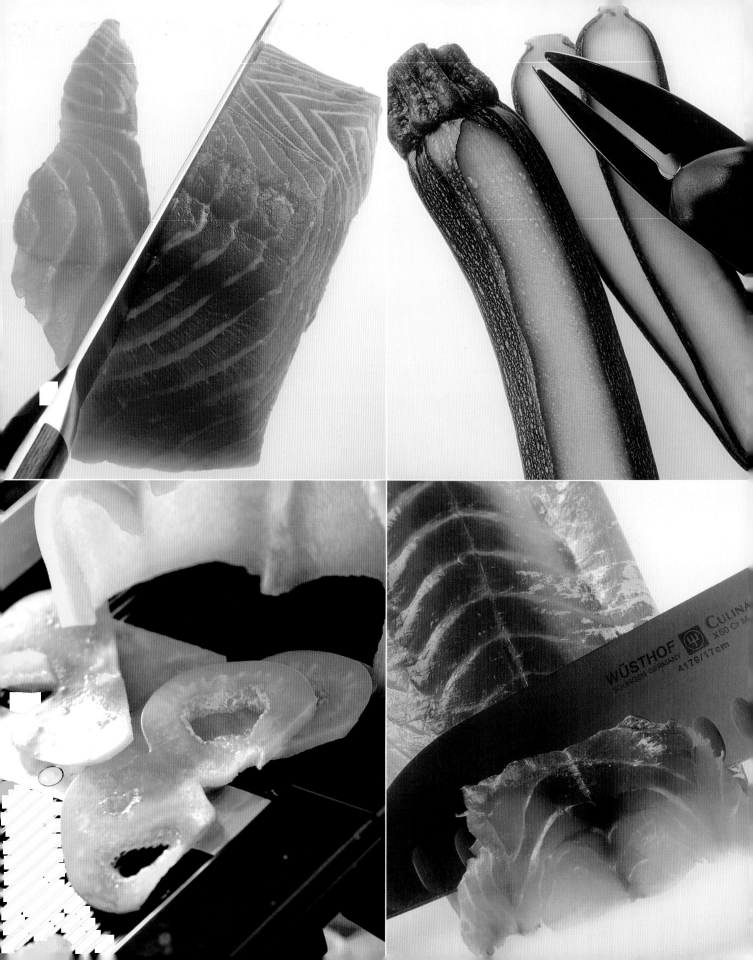

A short course in chopping

Good tools are the key to good performance: an effective knife revolutionises your cooking. Here are a few tips to put into practice (and give some tired ideas the chop).

ESSENTIAL BLADES

• A chef's knife for cutting meat, slicing vegetables and chopping herbs.

• A paring knife with a short blade for scraping or finely chopping fruit, vegetables, garlic or spices.

• A peeler for peeling fruits and vegetables (not too much though).

• A serrated bread knife, which is also good for cutting cakes without squashing them, and anything that has a soft centre.

ALL ABOARD

Always cut with the food placed flat on a board: chefs always practise their dexterity on a flat surface, whether a wooden or synthetic material.

THE WORD FROM THE CHEF

The more a blade is sharpened or ground, the better it will do its job. The aim is to make a clean cut that doesn't tear at the fibres of the food. This contributes to the textural integrity of the food and the pleasure of its preparation and eating.

Each to their own
Don't use the same knife (or board) for cutting raw meat and chopping up vegetables, as bacteria will be carried from one to the other.

THE WORD FROM THE EXPERT
It's better not to put your knives in the dishwasher, as this will dull the blade. And it's a good idea to wash and dry them straight away to avoid the risk of rust.

Sushi:
too easy

Easy to make at home, you'll need three basic ingreditents: rice (short-grain, preferably Japanese), special sushi vinegar and very good fish.

Use a special short-grain rice with a matching special sushi vinegar. Rinse the rice until the water runs clear, then drain. Place the rice in a saucepan and cover with one-and-a-half times its volume in water. Cover with a lid and bring to the boil. Once boiled, reduce the heat to low and cook for 15–20 minutes until *al dente*. The final touch: increase the heat to high for 10 seconds, then remove from the heat. Let the rice rest, still covered, for 10 minutes, then put into a large mixing bowl. Dissolve a little salt and sugar in the vinegar. Stir gently through the warm rice. Spread the rice out on a large plastic tray and allow to cool to room temperature.

Your fresh fish fillets should be skinless, and pin-boned. Train yourself to cut the fillets cleanly, with one movement, rather than sawing back and forth. Cut the pieces to 8 × 2.5cm and about 1cm thick. Wet your hands in a bowl of water, shape the cooled rice into elongated balls, add a dab of wasabi, a sliver of fish, and top with a band of seaweed. If using powdered wasabi, make a small heap and add water drop by drop to make a paste.

Freeze to be safe
Buy your fish ultra fresh and put it in the freezer immediately. That way, you preserve all of the taste while avoiding any risk of parasites.

From the oven
to the steamer

From steaming to baking, clever cooking brings together health benefits and energy savings.

COOKING WITH CARE

The steaming option is ideal for preserving the vitamins (and lovely colours) of delicate vegetables, or for cooking a whole chicken whose juices will slowly drip into the cooking water to make a fragrant broth. Scientifically designed cooking appliances for cooking with **gentle steam** are supposed to guarantee the maximum preservation of mineral salts, and even vitamin C, which cooking usually destroys. Use a non-stick **frying pan** to dry-sear foods without fat or oil. **Oven-tender** meat should be sealed for 5 minutes by browning it in a pan before roasting; this colours it on the outside while retaining all of its juices. Take care not to have the oven up too high; it breaks and toughens the meat fibres. The same goes for baking fish: fill a shallow tray with water and place in the bottom of the oven. This will transform it into a steam oven and prevent the flesh from drying out.

THE WORD FROM NATUROPATH AND CHEF LAURENCE SALOMON

Gently does it: there's too much heat in the kitchen! We're still being taught to bring oils and fats to smoking point— even though it's at that point, when the smoking point is reached, that the fatty acids deteriorate. Also, when the pot sputters too much, it's telling you something: things aren't okay. When cooking soup, gently simmer it, instead of having it at a rolling boil. And olive oil shouldn't be heated beyond **110°C**.

Wok in stock
A deliciously healthy way of cooking is to sear food with intense heat. The food cooks quickly, retaining its precious vitamins.

Grilling is great
Modern grilling options mean little (or no) oil.

Kitchen equipment:
gadgets to go

The right tools will change your life.
And take the chore out of cooking

SAUCEPANS: GOING TO POT

Saucepans and flameproof baking dishes in stainless steel with a heavy base distribute heat well and avoid oxidisation. Choose **durable non-stick materials**, which let you use a minimum of fat or oil, and slow-braise foods with very little liquid.

YOGHURT-MAKER

Reduce the billions of yoghurt tubs in landfill and make your own yoghurt. See page 191 for Laurence Salomon's recipe.

JUICE: A REAL HEALTH SPIN

Juice extractors are not necessarily very economical, but they are extremely satisfying. A blender allows you to make sauces, milkshakes, coulis and smoothies.

THE WORD FROM THE EXPERT
JUICE EXTRACTORS: THE ORGANIC VERSION
The slow grinding of 'masticating' juicers, based on the principle of chewing, is supposed to retain almost all the nutrients and microfibre of fruit and vegetables.

9
the secrets of female chefs

MODEL CHEFS

Fresh tomato and eggplant terrine (recipe opposite).

Baby calamari salad with tomatoes, beans and basil (recipe page 190).

Nadia Santini
Chef, *dal Pescatore*, Mantua, Italy

Fourth-in-command at restaurant dal Pescatore, in the heart of the Italian countryside, Nadia works alongside her husband Antonio's mother to reinvent a feminine cuisine, timeless and generous, that interprets modern trends with the lightest of touches.

"Kitchen steam is the best anti-wrinkle treatment!"

" Beauty? It's a form of magic that touches everyone's heart, while keeping an element of mystery at the same time. The harmony of forms, colours and styles makes it a pleasure that's higher than all others, which transcends culture, goes beyond ethnicity, class and borders. **In the kitchen, men and women practise the most beautiful profession in the world: speaking through their dishes, offering happiness and wellbeing, it's an accomplishment, a way of making the world a better place.** Men's cooking is all about imagination, the avant-garde, aesthetics… Women have, in addition, a sense of culture and a more romantic and maternal sensibility of the nurturing mother. A woman's unique approach is the need to offer something that's good for the health as well—to do otherwise would keep me awake at night! ▶

MY BEAUTY RECIPE
FRESH TOMATO AND EGGPLANT TERRINE

• I took some tomatoes, eggplant (aubergine), basil and its little white flowers from the garden to make a Caprese salad without the cheese. I peeled the eggplants, finely sliced them and fried them in a pan with some olive oil and a little salt and pepper. Then I lined the base and sides of a terrine.

• Precious vitamin C disappears with heat, so I peeled the tomatoes by hand and halved and squeezed them to get rid of their seeds and excess moisture. I lay them in the terrine with some stock to form a gel, plus a few basil leaves, then covered the top with some more eggplant and put it in the freezer.

• After 20 minutes, I cut 1.5cm thick slices and drizzled them with olive oil, then garnished with basil flowers and sea salt. Simplicity itself: the best things are often made with very few ingredients.

Nadia in the "vegetable garden" with Whisky.

▶ ## "MEN THINK OF OUR PROFESSION AS A WINDOW INTO THE WORLD, AND WOMEN AS A WINDOW INTO THE HEART."

"Globalisation is a movement that tries to erase historical differences and individuality—for me, this has to be a springboard towards a new humanism. History is made up of highs and lows, but you can encourage evolution, offer a new form of wealth. No to homogenisation! Italian cooking, direct and simple, has left its mark on the world while safeguarding its heritage at the same time—it has a wealth of exchanges and identities tied to its European culture, from the Mediterranean to Africa. In *The Decameron*, **Bocaccio was, in 1350, celebrating parmesan cheese and tortellini!** Knowledge is passed down over centuries, tradition is only the sum of tiny innovations—what a wonderful inheritance. Vive la différence! In Europe, you only have to travel 60km, two hours on a bicycle, to find an incredible variety of dishes and traditions—whereas you need to travel eight hours on a plane in America. Big cities homogenise all that, but it still exists in the countryside. We've experienced it between Lyon and Roanne, from chefs the Troisgros brothers to Paul Bocuse. In the restaurants of the greats, the Haeberlin family, Roger Vergé, Raymond Blanc, we appreciated the demonstrations of love expressed in their cooking. Cooking is like theatre: you expect emotions, authenticity, the flavours of the imagination and the reflection of strong roots and new energies. It's knowledge that lets you appreciate the differences.

"**During your honeymoon, you have to put away stores of sweetness and harvest the maximum amount of honey, for the rest of your life.** Chefs have a classical education that serves as the foundation of their own avant-garde methods, a way of cooking that's been proven over centuries of experience—by preserving life. They have the knowledge, the ethics and the spirit to offer health and wellbeing. What could be a more positive foundation? Technology can be the worst of things but also the best, and be used to serve healthy ends. Take the Pacojet, for example, a machine that lets you make express granitas, emulsify raw or frozen substances (even ice cubes) and whip air into them—and even make sorbets without sugar.

Health foods influence traditional recipes in subtle ways, without distorting them. In her book *A History of Food*, Maguelonne Toussaint-Samat tells the story of King Theuderic I in Byzantium asking a famous Greek doctor whether the best way to apply the principles of healthy nutrition was through recipes: he went on to found a school at Salerno that laid the foundations of our gastronomic culture."

MY FAVOURITE BEAUTY PRODUCTS

Cooking is like a symphony with infinite variations, even if, just like music, you only start with seven notes. I have the privilege of living in the country, in tune with nature, time and the seasons. **Our kitchen garden** is a nursery of treasures that offers year-round happiness. There are new surprises every day. The summer tomatoes that go into the winter preserves, the cep mushrooms in autumn… Baby lettuces, the radishes at the end of winter and the new peas of spring… The March saffron that makes a wonderful risotto. We appreciate everything, even winter. I adore grapefruit, orange or peach juices, and a green tea from Mauritius with lemon, but I also appreciate the taste of teas and infusions—we have lemon verbena trees in the garden, an amazing perfume, and we use it a lot in our desserts.

"**And the beauty that comes out of the ovens**. Their 'good' humidity keeps the face clear of wrinkles. I work in the kitchen with **my 80-year-old mother-in-law and she has the skin of a young girl!**"

MY BEAUTY RECIPE
PEACH AND CHERRY COMPOTE
WITH A BERRY INFUSION
- 500 ml water • 350 ml dry white wine
- ⅓ cup sugar • juice of half a lemon
- 4 peaches • ½ cup berries • 12 cherries

Place the water, wine, sugar and lemon juice in a saucepan and bring to the boil. Add the peaches and the berries and simmer for 4–5 minutes (depending on the size of the peaches). Remove from the heat, add the cherries and allow to cool. Peel the peaches, cut them up, including the kernel, and immerse them in the infusion. Serve in a shallow bowl with some of the berry infusion.
See page 190 for more of Nadia's recipes.

Beef tartare
(recipe
opposite).

Rougui Dia
Chef, *Petrossian*, Paris

Since 2005, 32-year-old Rougui Dia has been a chef at Petrossian, one of the Parisian temples of caviar, whose reputation has spread as far as New York. This stunning French woman, of Senegalese origin, embodies a new generation of cooks, open to all the flavours of the world.

"I travel a lot in order to discover flavours and share them."

Beauty is about generosity, about what you exude when you're comfortable in your own skin and what people want to capture, even if it can't necessarily be defined, and there's something wonderful about that. There are different facets to beauty, whether you're curvy or not, you're fine as you are, there's no need to judge. Thinner girls think: 'I wish I was more shapely'—and vice-versa. We're never happy! We don't make the same demands on men. So I say to the men in the kitchen: 'I've given you all a mark between zero to ten', just to see their reactions.

Beauty affects the palate as well: women are all about subtlety. So, even when using spices, everything is handled gently." ▶

MY 'HYPERPROTEIN' BEAUTY RECIPE

BEEF TARTARE
- 560g minced beef • salt • pepper
- 2 teaspoon sesame seeds
- 2 pinches hot paprika
- 1 tablespoon crushed roasted hazelnuts • 200ml sherry vinegar
- 100ml olive oil • 20g farmed caviar
- Chervil sprigs and toasted flatbread

Place the minced beef, salt, pepper, sesame seeds, paprika, crushed hazelnuts and sherry vinegar in a bowl and combine the mixture well. Incorporate the olive oil little by little.
Spread the mixture on a tray and use a cutter to create circles. Arrange on a plate, alternating a layer of tartare and a layer of caviar.
Place a quenelle of caviar on top of each stack. Sprinkle a little paprika around and garnish with a few sprigs of chervil and the flatbread.

Bream fillets with lemon vodka sauce and quinoa (recipe page 190).

▶ "We also want lighter dishes: enjoying yourself is also about feeling good when you leave the table, with the feeling of having eaten well, not feeling bloated, sleepy or guilty—it's important, when you think about everything a woman has to handle these days. Dishes with a lot of sauce don't suit our lifestyle anymore. That style of cooking is more compatible with intense activity. It's an awareness that's developed naturally.

"**Having several different cultures** in the one restaurant is very enriching. Because Mr Petrossian, a Parisian Armenian who often goes to the United States, is very open and travels a lot—just like me—we're tasting new ingredients all the time. **I was born in France and I'm discovering my Senegalese background, but also the whole African continent (Morocco, for example)**. I draw different flavours from these places, which are then mingled with French cuisine, the foundation of our menu, delicately enriched with new notes. A lovely assemblage of flavours, spicy but not hot—spice can be confused with pepperiness. It's very easy to make flavours that are overly strong, too harsh; it's a lot less easy to transform an ingredient while keeping its personality. Every ingredient has its place, nothing is hidden or masked. So, for example, I combine the very sour **tamarind,** which you find in India and Africa, with orange in a vinaigrette to soften it. Served with crispy prawn parcels, it takes you on a journey.

"I LIKE TO START A NEW DAY LIKE YOU IMAGINE A NEW RECIPE."

"And it's important to take time for yourself. My anti-stress formula is African dancing—for the breathing and smiling that's an important part of it, like a kind of gift to others.

What can you do for your body to feel good without having to resort to medicine? I adore vegetables! Broccoli cooked in a very small amount of water, carrots, lentils, parsley—all of these naturally offer lots of vitamins. When I'm feeling tired this is my antidote. The challenge is to make them tempting to eat—in a different form. Don't get stuck on the idea that you don't like such or such. When I was little, I didn't enjoy cooked witlof very much, which I found very bitter. And then my cousin who got me into professional cooking offered me some to taste—it was a completely different thing! Sliced thinly, in a little butter and orange juice, with scallops, it's perfect. Since then, it's been my mission to make even the most reluctant love them! Turnips, simmered, then caramelised in sweet butter… green peas with coconut milk—I've even converted one of my sisters!

"**In cooking, be gentle with everything**, add only a very small amount of water to preserve the vitamins. All of my dishes are cooked very quickly to retain their flavour and freshness—and the green of young vegetables."

"All my dishes are cooked very quickly in very little water to preserve the vitamins."

MY FAVOURITE BEAUTY PRODUCTS

"**Caviar** is a subtle and delicate product—with a touch of iodine, a very intriguing nuttiness and an incredible delicacy. The eggs burst beneath the palate, and give an enormous amount of flavour. It's

a delight for our tastebuds, but it has other virtues as well: its use in cosmetics comes from purely practical observations. **People who handle caviar have very beautiful hands,** with very fine-textured skin. Madame Petrossian mentioned it to one of her customers who was working for Ingrid Millet—who developed one of the first hand creams. It resulted in a beauty cream; putting it on the skin gives a 'lifting' effect that has been explored in the laboratory. You only need to put some on your skin to experience the pore-tightening effect due to the action of the vitamins contained in the eggs, and the genetic complexity of their chemical make-up. The sturgeon is one of the most ancient fish in the world; they're thought to be 300 million years old. Each is recognised within the one species by its particular DNA. It's so rich that you can combine the action of the egg with heat or cold—avenues that still haven't been explored yet. **Research is underway to look at other applications (on hair, for example). Why not a Beluga shampoo**?

"**Pomegranate**, Eve's 'apple' was, in fact, the fruit of God. The proof? The number of seeds it contains is divisible by 33. I use pomegranate juice in the same way as balsamic vinegar, or in cooking, in the caramelised turkey fillets with pomegranate, for example (recipe page 190)."

*Mille-feuille
of fish and
vegetables
(recipe opposite).*

*Mussels served
with quality
homemade
french fries,
cooked in
single-use
vegetable oil,
lighten the
nutritional
bottom line.*

Ghislaine Arabian
Chef, *Les Petites Sorcières*, Paris

The first female chef in France to achieve two Michelin stars (in 1987), Ghislaine Arabian, following the very prestigious Pavillon Ledoyen, has opened 'her' Parisian bistro, Les Petites Sorcières. It's a cuisine that's magic in its simplicity. Proud of her Flemish roots, she is motivated by pleasure: "My choices in life, like my choices in what I eat, are made according to what inspires me."

"Combining beauty and cooking has become something that's obvious."

" Beauty is the detail that makes the difference; it's a smile, not plastic perfection. **The most amazing elixir won't work if the mind doesn't follow: everything hinges on mental attitude, which is inseparable from the health of the body. It's your mood that gives you lovely skin and eyes that shine**. We're always chasing after something, whereas it's really all about balance. Strive for wellbeing, with some thought given to the figure; aesthetic issues will always be in the foreground, guided by conscious health concerns. But it's a reflex, to train yourself to pay attention to the balance. A woman in the kitchen must necessarily keep this balance in mind. Combining beauty and cooking has become something that's obvious. It hasn't always been the case: it's connected to the resurgence of organic produce, through plants and fruits,

▶

MY BEAUTY RECIPE

MILLE-FEUILLE OF FISH AND VEGETABLES
• A recipe that can be made all year round, varying the vegetables according to the season.
• Summer: eggplant (aubergine), tomato, zucchini (courgette), capsicum (pepper).
• Winter: cabbage, carrots, leeks.
• Autumn: wild mushrooms.
• Spring: peas, asparagus and artichokes.
Thinly slice the fish and place on a baking tray and drizzle with olive or grapeseed oil and salt and pepper.
Bake for a few seconds in a preheated hot oven.
Thinly slice the vegetables and steam or simmer until just cooked.
Layer the fish and vegetables.
Serve with a light olive oil, lemon vinaigrette and seasonal herbs with finely diced summer tomatoes, if in season.

MODEL CHEFS

"My daughter Margaux was eating raw scampi and oysters at four months!"

▶ and a personal journey related to common sense, to what's natural. Cucumber on the eyes, rose and cornflower water, honey, clay, are elementary products expressing all of a women's wisdom.

"Plants and fruits, vegetables and flowers have essential properties that we're now rediscovering scientifically, but which were already known through experience, instinctively. Our diet gets worse and worse, and at the same time we stuff ourselves with vitamin pills and other supplements—whereas it's all there in food, in a natural state. It's the combination of foods that provides the right balance.

"**I eat in an intuitive way; you have to know how to listen to your body. And without being harassed by the doctor. It's second nature, putting health into your cooking**. We're losing our good sense because of the abundance of produce all year round—we need to get back to our food rhythms. Beginning with choosing fruits and vegetables in season, not just because they taste better, but because our body asks for them at that time. Our biological cycles correspond to the cycles of natural production.

"**We need the diuretic properties of asparagus at the end of winter, and protective foods that heat us up, such as walnut oil (an extraordinary product). Consider cabbage**, whose nutrient analysis shows that not only is it low in calories but that it provides nutrients at a time when we are most deficient. Use in sauerkraut, as a salad, cooked or raw, stuffed, or in all its forms. Apples, onions and red cabbage make wonderful accompaniments. Eat artichokes, which are so good for the liver; potatoes for their potassium; celeriac with its nutty taste; mushrooms, delightful raw, with lemon, a little cream, salt and pepper. As for witlof, it balances the richness of what it is served with and because it is full of water, it's satisfying, but you can eat a kilo of it. As for vegetables that are available all year round, there's the wonderful spinach, but it must be eaten fresh, not reheated, or else their oxalic acid comes out. And then there's sorrel and leek, excellent against cholesterol and for regularity; in summer or winter, it's a foundation to which you add something seasonal.

Eat carrots for a good complexion. When my daughter, Margaux, was born, I gave her carrot juice in summer, cooked in winter and she always had a wonderful colour. I never gave her cooked butter, I fed her steamed fish with a drizzle of olive oil. She never ate little jars of baby food—because I wasn't giving her any sugar. She was brought up in the kitchen: she was eating raw scampi and oysters at four months! We ate raw food, well before the fashion for sushi. We don't deprive ourselves, but we are all slim: the habit is instilled. There's no need for sweets. Sugar is already in food, so why add more? I know that if I crave sugar, it's a sign of an energy slump that will pass, an unconscious call for fast sugars."

BEETROOT OR BERRIES, MY CRAVINGS ARE NEVER OUT OF STEP WITH THE SEASONS

"Oranges, for example: all the elements they contain, with vitamin C at the top of the list, correspond to the body's needs in winter. At home, we always ate them at Christmas, a marvellous perfume mingled with the aroma of the *pain d'épices* we had for afternoon tea with mashed banana and molasses. When cooking I prefer to add **a spoonful of cream instead of butter because it has much**

less fat. The best chips aren't fatty [and are] made with frying oil that's changed every two uses. **And then it's all a matter of what you have with them: with mussels, which are ultra-healthy**, it's a feast that doesn't sit heavily on the stomach. It's better to eat homemade fries than crisps or processed snack foods. **I make a chocolate mousse without yolks, butter or sugar, just with egg whites (excellent for the muscles) and dark 70 per cent chocolate (a balm for the soul). It's all good!** Just like my homemade jam with just 30 per cent sugar."

MY FAVOURITE BEAUTY PRODUCTS

"**Summer tomatoes** are essential ingredients. A pure marvel with their mineral salts. I keep **preserved lemon** in the refrigerator all year round (15 days in salted water with a little sugar and lots of bay leaves), as well as **parsley** (a treasure that grows even in winter, it's no accident it's available the whole year). And **fresh ginger**: it's tempting, it stimulates your appetite and makes you happy. I grate it and add it to everything! And no need for ready-made chutney-style preparations: fresh mango, bought at the market, chopped up in a fish sauce in winter—or in a meat jus. No glutamate, no hidden sugar, an exotic touch, all natural."

Seaweed salad and grilled mullet (recipe page 191).

Date dessert (recipe opposite and continued page 191).

Laurence Salomon
Chef, *Nature et Saveur*, Annecy

The first chef to promote the Originelle® cuisine, which brings together, in gourmet style, the values of organic food and respect for local produce, creativity and the refusal of the unnatural, Laurence Salomon, with her naturopath's expertise is a genuine pioneer. Her restaurant was awarded the Laurier Ecorismo 2008 for her contribution to this gentle, and delicious, revolution.

"Cooking in tune with our physiology is a vital development!"

Saying that how I eat influences my health and my looks is simply common and good sense.

If I eat just anything, after a week I have spots! You have to stay authentic, as close to nature as possible. Why are so few chefs concerned with these issues? You understand it if you look at the professional course to get your chef's certificate: the recipes, the course material, it's all very removed from current priorities. At a time when we know we have to learn how to remove the sugar from desserts, the program still has them making a *tarte Bourdaloue* with pears preserved in syrup, and too much butter and sugar. The revolution still hasn't reached the catering colleges; there's an enormous lag behind what some chefs are actually doing. There's an educational deficiency." ▶

MY BEAUTY RECIPE

DATE DESSERT
Date pudding
- 15 pitted Medjool dates • 1 litre oat milk • 1 tablespoon hazelnut liqueur
- 1 tablespoon arrowroot
- 1 teaspoon agar agar powder
- Large pinch ground cinnamon

Date cream
- 5 pitted Medjool dates
- 2 pinches ground cinnamon

To make the date pudding, process 13 dates with half of the oat milk, liqueur, arrowroot, agar agar and cinnamon. Pour into a heavy-based saucepan, add the remaining oat milk and cook, whisking, until it comes to the boil. Reduce the heat to low and cook, stirring, for another 3 minutes. Pour into ramekins, cool, cover with plastic wrap and refrigerate until chilled. To make the date cream, process the dates in a blender with the cinnamon and enough water to form a paste. **Continued page 191**

*Chicken strips
with ginger
(recipe page 191).*

"I am a self-taught cook; I had never cooked outside my own home and I started by giving courses in cooking and nutrition to individuals as well as professionals. **I went to teach the team of the great chef, Régis Marcon, a three-star chef and a pioneer in the field of sustainable development**. I ordered all organic groceries, vegetables, meats and fish and I did demonstrations of sweet and savoury dishes for them: **it was a very different approach, very disorienting for them**. Not using butter in cooking, for example, changes everything.

"**I am not against butter, when it is made from raw milk — and used raw**. Pasteurised butter has lost its lactic flora, and saprophytic organisms. As soon as you cook it, it's no longer as digestible. In a dégustation menu, you can find yourself served with a series of dishes containing hidden butter, baby vegetables glazed with butter, butter here, butter there, until dessert. And all of that will sit heavily. **I cook without butter and without cream**. In a lemon tart, I replace the butter with a raw-milk goat's cheese *faisselle*. For a béchamel sauce, I start off with olive oil and add soy milk to finish. And I use oat or rice milk for my crème anglaise."

THERE'S NOTHING HARDER THAN CHANGING YOUR FOOD HABITS

"**Wheat gluten**, public enemy number one? No, it's just that we didn't eat wheat so much before. But today, industrial producers only use flours that no longer rise, because they're so impoverished. Because it's the gluten that's the 'bread-making' ingredient, they add extra. And because these flours are tasteless, they've started over-salting bread, making bubble-gum flours that are very high, too high, in gluten. Hence the problems with intolerance. **Good bread** depends on the quality of the flour (semi-wholemeal and not white)—and the baker! There are alternatives to industrially produced wheat, which has become GSO (genetically selected organism, made incompatible with our metabolism. Stoneground *einkorn* wheat, a T80-type flour, yellow and high in beta carotene, is the most natural. The electrical millstones, unlike cylinders used in stone ground, don't remove the germ or the aleurone layer, which lets you digest the wheat properly. A mill grinds 30–40 kg an hour, while a cylinder several tonnes! As for sourdough, it predigests the gluten and counterbalances the acidity of certain wholemeal flours—as long as it is pure (only 1 per cent yeast is needed to take over the fermentation time). Eating buckwheat all the time is no better. It's the too-high dose that makes the poison."

MY FAVOURITE BEAUTY PRODUCTS

"**The fresh seaweed salad** (recipe page 191) keeps for six days in the refrigerator, and goes with fish or vegetable dishes. The dry-seaweed mixtures in flakes can also be easily incorporated into different dishes. Seaweed is high in trace elements, including iodine. And, according to the SU.VI.MAX study, insufficient iodine intake is responsible for significant biological imbalances or problems (delayed mental development, lower fertility and miscarriage). And yet we don't need very much: 150 µg per day, or 30mg dried seaweed or 210 mg fresh seaweed. They regulate the thyroid gland, which governs our basal metabolism and influences bodyweight, if they are eaten regularly.

The high levels of living and active bacteria in yoghurts fermented with lactobacillus, acidophilus and bifidus makes them extremely beneficial. They improve the digestibility of milk proteins; the calcium that's made soluble by lactic acid is more easily assimilated and the level of group B vitamins increases from 15 to 20 per cent. Making your own yoghurts from whole organic milk and a strain of bifidus lets you take advantage of their benefits and give a lighter texture (commercial producers systematically add powdered skim milk).

To make **vanilla-flavoured soy yoghurt** you'll need a yoghurt-maker. Empty the contents of 1 small tub of plain soy yoghurt in a container with a pouring lip, gradually add 1 litre vanilla soy milk, whisking constantly. Pour into pots, close the yoghurt-maker and plug it in. About eight hours later, remove the yoghurt pots, cover immediately with lids and put them in the refrigerator. If you make it with plain soy milk, you will get the equivalent of the thick lacto-fermented soy creams, more suitable for using in savoury dishes. See the recipe on page 191 to make yoghurt from cow's milk."

WANT TO EAT HEALTHY? THEN GET BACK TO THE STOVE! A DIFFERENT CULINARY PATH IS POSSIBLE; THE FUTURE IS IN AUTHENTICITY.

"Use ingredients that are as unprocessed as possible, paying attention to impostors. Always read the label on organic foods carefully to check their certifiction and make sure you get what you're paying for. And be consciious of how much waste you make. In my restaurant, we only 'produce' one garbage bag a day."

MODEL RECIPES

ROUGUI DIA

MY TURKEY ESCALOPES WITH POMEGRANATE JUICE

• 5 slices turkey fillet
• 700ml pomegranate juice
• 5 cloves • 10g juniper berries
• 20ml olive oil • 50g French shallots
• 2 tablespoons butter
• 1kg carrots, sliced into rounds
• 20 g sugar • salt • pepper
• 200g streaky bacon pieces

Marinate the turkey fillets in the pomegranate juice and spices overnight. Heat the olive oil in a large frying pan over medium heat and cook the turkey until browned on each side. Add the shallots, marinating juice and cook until thickened.
Melt the butter in a large frying pan and cook the carrots until tender. Season with sugar and salt.
Cook the bacon until crispy.
To serve, arrange the turkey on the carrots, top with the bacon and spoon over the sauce.

BREAM FILLETS WITH LEMON VODKA SAUCE AND QUINOA (pictured page 180)
Serves 4

• 7cm piece of leek • 1 carrot, halved
• 10g butter • 200g quinoa
Lemon vodka sauce
• 250ml lemon vodka • 100ml lemon juice
• 60ml cream • 4 bream fillets
• 20ml olive oil • salt and pepper

Peel, wash and julienne the vegetables. Place in a saucepan with the butter and 2 tablespoons water and simmer over low heat until tender.
Place the quinoa in a saucepan of lightly salted water, bring to the boil and simmer until tender.
To make the lemon vodka sauce, simmer the vodka until reduced by half. Add the lemon juice and a pinch of salt, simmer for another 5 minutes, then add the cream.
Season the bream with salt and pepper. Heat the olive oil in a large frying pan over high heat and cook skin-side down until crispy, then reduce heat to medium-low and cook the other side for 2–3 minutes. Serve on top of the julienne of vegetables with the sauce poured around and the quinoa in a small dish.

NADIA SANTINI

BABY CALAMARI SALAD WITH TOMATOES, BEANS AND BASIL (pictured page 174)
Serves 4

• Cook a handful of fresh white beans in cold water with a spoonful of olive oil, black peppercorns and a pinch of salt for 10 minutes or until tender. Drain.
• Wash the calamari well, then poach in boiling water with a little lemon juice for 15 seconds. Rinse them under cold water to stop them cooking further.
• Combine the beans; calamari; 1 peeled, seeded and finely diced tomato; basil leaves; extra-virgin olive oil; and sharpen with some lemon and a little pepper. With good tomatoes from Sardinia or Sicily, I never add salt, as they are naturally salty.

PIGEON-STUFFED RAVIOLI
Serves 4

• To make the filling, heat 1 tablespoon olive oil in a small frying pan over low heat. Add 1 teaspoon each of finely chopped French shallot, celery and carrot and cook until soft. Add the finely chopped meat of 1 pigeon or quail and stir for 2 minutes. Add 1 tablespoon white wine and 2 tablespoons chicken stock and bring to a simmer. Season with salt, pepper and finely chopped rosemary. Process in a blender until smooth.
• To make the pasta, make a dough using 200g flour, 3 egg yolks, 1 egg white and 1 tablespoon spinach purée. Roll out the dough into thin sheets and cut into squares. Place a teaspoon of filling on each square, fold the pasta over and press edges to seal well.
• Cook for 2–3 minutes in chicken stock and serve with pan-fried mushrooms.

LAURENCE SALOMON

TOFU MILLE-FEUILLES WITH SPINACH (pictured page 66)
Serves 4

• 600g spinach leaves
• salt
• 500g firm tofu
• 60ml shoyu (Japanese soy sauce)
• 60ml olive oil
• 1 teaspoon caraway seeds
• pinch dried herbs
• baby spinach leaves
Shallot rice
• 4 French shallots, finely chopped
• 2 tablespoons olive oil
• salt
• 150g brown basmati rice
• 1 teaspoon vegetable stock powder
Orange cardamom emulsion
• 1 orange
• 2 tablespoons olive oil
• 10 cardamom seeds

To make the shallot rice, gently sauté the shallot with olive oil and a few pinches of salt. Rinse the rice, drain it and add to the shallot. Combine the stock powder with 200ml water and add to the rice. Cover and cook over low heat for 30 minutes.
To make the orange cardamom emulsion, remove the peel and pith from the orange and then remove the segments. Set aside. Process the peel, olive oil, cardamom seeds and a pinch of salt in a blender until smooth. Add enough water to make a thick emulsion.
Wash the spinach, but don't dry it. Place in a large frying pan, cover and cook for 5 minutes or until just wilted. Drain, then squeeze out the moisture. Finely chop and season with salt.
Cut the tofu into 12 thin slices. Place 4 slices on an oven tray. Drizzle over some shoyu and olive oil and sprinkle with a few caraway seeds. Spread a thin layer of spinach over the slices and cover with 4 more tofu slices. Pour over some more shoyu and olive oil and sprinkle with herbs. Repeat with remaining shoyu, olive oil, spinach and caraway seeds.
Bake the mille-feuilles at 170°C for 10 minutes or until just heated through. Place a few baby spinach leaves and the orange segments on plates. Place the mille-feuilles on top, spoon over some shallot rice and drizzle over the orange cardamom emulsion.

Nadia Santini's pigeon-stuffed ravioli (recipe page 190).

CHICKEN STRIPS WITH GINGER
(pictured page 188)
Serves 4

- 3 chicken breast fillets, thinly sliced
- ½ green capsicum (pepper), thinly sliced
- 1 small yellow zucchini (courgette), cut into sticks
- ¼ teaspoon grated ginger
- 1 tablespoon tamari
- 80ml olive oil
- pinch dried herbs
- 250g quinoa spaghetti
- salt
- 30g red quinoa
- 15 hazelnuts

Hazelnut oil cream

- 5 sprigs parsley, finely chopped
- 1 small garlic clove, finely chopped
- 100ml plain soy milk
- 50ml hazelnut oil
- few drops lemon juice
- salt

Combine the chicken, capsicum, zucchini, ginger, tamari, 2 tablespoons olive oil and the dried herbs in a shallow container and toss to coat well. Allow to marinate in the refrigerator for a few hours.

To make the hazelnut oil cream, place the parsley and garlic in a blender with the soy milk, hazelnut oil and a few pinches of salt. Blend for 20 seconds, then add the lemon juice.

Cook the spaghetti in a large saucepan of salted boiling water for 10 minutes. Drain, reserving a spoonful of the cooking water. Return the spaghetti to the pan, add 1 tablespoon olive oil and the reserved cooking water and combine. Meanwhile, cook the quinoa in three times its volume of salted water for 20 minutes or until tender.

Coarsely chop the hazelnuts, then place in a non-stick pan and shake over medium heat until lightly toasted. Set aside.

To cook the chicken strips, heat the remaining olive oil in a wok until very hot, then cook the chicken, in batches until cooked through.

To serve, arrange a bed of spaghetti on each plate, lay the chicken strips on top and scatter with quinoa and toasted hazelnuts and serve with the hazelnut oil cream.

SEAWEED SALAD AND GRILLED MULLET
(pictured page 186)
Serves 4

Grilled mullet

- 8 red mullet fillets
- few pinches five spice
- salt

Fresh seaweed salad

- 100g fresh dulse seaweed
- 50g fresh wakame
- 50g fresh sea lettuce
- 50g fresh brown algae (kelp)
- 2 French shallots, finely chopped
- juice of 1 lemon
- 1 teaspoon dried herbs
- sesame oil
- salt

Sea lettuce emulsion

- 80g fresh sea lettuce
- 45ml sesame oil
- 30ml lemon juice
- salt

To make the seaweed salad, wash each kind of seaweed in several lots of water to remove the salt. Drain and squeeze them well to remove the water, then chop and place in a shallow container. Combine the shallot and lemon juice. Add to the seaweed with the dried herbs and and enough sesame oil to coat the seaweed well. Cover and refrigerate until well chilled.

To make the sea lettuce emulsion, wash the sea lettuce and place in a blender with the other ingredients. Blend, adding enough water to obtain an emulsion that coats the back of a spoon.

To make the grilled mullet, sprinkle the fish with the five spice and salt. Arrange skin-side up a lightly oiled baking tray and cook under a hot grill until just cooked through.

To serve, serve the fish with a spoonful of fresh seaweed salad and a drizzle of seaweed emulsion.

DATE DESSERT
(continued from page 187)
Hazelnut cream

- 2 tablespoons plain hazelnut purée
- 1 tablespoon rice syrup

To make the hazelnut cream, process the hazelnut purée with the rice syrup in a blender until smooth, then add enough water to make a sauce thick enough to coat the back of a spoon.

To serve, place a spoonful of date cream on each plate. Unmould each dessert onto the plates and top with a spoonful of hazelnut cream and the remaining sliced dates.

COW'S MILK YOGHURT

- 250 ml full-cream plain yoghurt
- 1 litre full-cream cow's milk
- 1 yoghurt-maker (optional)

Place the yoghurt in a container with a pouring lip and gradually add the milk while whisking continually.

If using a yoghurt maker, pour into pots, close the lid and turn it on. Around 8 hours later, remove the yoghurt pots, cover them immediately with their lids and refrigerate.

If you don't have a yoghurt maker, you can use a simple casserole dish instead. To do this, place the yoghurt-filled pots in the dish, pour in hot water to come up to the top of the pots, cover and stand for 8 hours at room temperature. You can flavour the yoghurt with a few drops of vanilla extract or a good jam or a few drops of essential lemon or sweet orange oil.

Credits

PHOTOGRAPHER CREDITS

Jean-Claude Amiel (p. 7a, 60b, 106a) ; **Barbro Andersson** (p. 99) ; **Martyn Antonson** (p. 17, 24-25, 157) ; **Alexis Armanet** (p. 171) ; **Atelier Berdoy et Arcadius** (p. 29) ; **Jean-Luc Barde** (p. 104) ; **Aloïs Beer** (p. 124a, 141, 173) ; **Jérôme Bilic** (p. 35, 109, 137) ; **Isabelle Bonjean/Made** (p. 48) ; **Pierre Cabannes** (p. 66c) ; **Thierry Cambier et DR** (p. 182 à 185) ; **Nathalie Carnet** (p. 145) ; **Edouard Chauvin** (p.146); **Cliff Chen** (p. 21, 64) ; **Collection Petrossian (Ch. Charzat – M.Schlegel)** (p. 178 à 181) ; **Tim Evan Cook** (p. 85b) ; **Capucine de Chabaneix** (p. 148) ; **Gilles de Chabaneix** (p. 28, 58c, 112, 150) ; **Pierre-Emmanuel Dehais** (p. 18) ; **Thomas Dhellemmes** (p. 103a) ; **Frédéric Farré** (couverture; p. 27) ; **Christine Fleurent** (p. 55, 61b, 106b, 106c) ; **Eric Flogny/Aleph (Angel des Montagnes)** (p. 14) ; **Guillaume Girardot** (p. 51, 90, 124b) ; **Valery Guedes** (p. 58a) ; **Francis Hammond** (p. 56b, 57a, 72b); **Emmanuelle Hauguel** (p. 44) ; **Gilles Hirgorom** (p. 7e, 32c, 37c, 68a, 103c) ; **Pierre Hussenot** (p. 36b) ; **Eddy Kohli** (p. 52) ; **Sylvie Lancrenon** (p. 39, 163) ; **François Lange** (p. 43) ; **Guillaume de Laubier** (p. 6b, 73b, 161); **Laurence Salomon** (p. 162); **Valérie Lhomme** (p. 84a, 89, 153); **Jean-Jacques Magis** (p. 83a, 143); **Marie Claire Hong Kong/South China Media** (p. 76, 96); **André Martin** (p. 66a, 94b, 95b); **P. Martin** (p. 86b); **Eric Matheron-Balay** (p. 142); **Marc Montezin** (p. 30, 40, 100, 170); **Marie-Pierre Morel** (p. 103b); **Alain Muriot** (p. 56c, 86a); **Loïc Nicoloso** (p. 70b); **Bob Norris** (p. 140); **Patrick Parchet** (p. 75 **Guy Pascal** (p. 73a); **Pedro studio photo**, avec l'autorisation des **éditions Grancher** (p. 66b, 186 à 189); **Frédéric Pine** (p. 110); **Bruno Poinsard** (p. 120); **Jean-François Rivière** (p. 80, 84b) ; **Robert Erdmann/ August/ Acte 2** (p. 26 **Virginie Rol** (p. 116c); **Laurent Rouvrais** (p. 6j, 9, 33a, 37b, 57b, 61a, 94c, 95a, 122, 135, 154, 155, 160, 164c, 166a, 166b, 167, 169); **Corinne Ryman** (p. 33b); **Philippe Scaf** (p. 174 à 177, 190-191); **Manfred Seelow** (p. 6i, 32a, 32b, 34a, 36a, 54a, 54c, 56a, 58b, 67a, 67b, 69b, 70a, 71a, 71b, 72a, 73c, 73d, 79, 83b, 85a, 85c, 87b, 94a, 116b, 116a, 117, 118, 119, 121, 125, 126a, 126b, 126c, 127, 129, 130, 131, 133, 134, 136, 138, 149, 152, 159, 164a, 164b, 164d, 168); **Patrick Swirc** (p. 156); **Lamb Taylor** (p. 10); **Hervé This** (p. 20); **Jean-Charles Vaillant** (p. 34c, 60a, 69a, 93, 107); **Christoph Valentin** (p. 34b, 68b); **Cees Van Gelderen** (p. 47); **Jose Van Riele** (p. 59); **Philippe Vaures Santa Maria** (p. 113); **Pierre Louis Viel** (p. 37b); **Sarah Wels** (p. 6d, 22); **Bernhard inkelmann** (p. 54b, 63, 87a); **Michael Wooley** (p. 13).

MODEL CREDITS

CRYSTAL-Sandrine Vargas (p. 18) ; **ELITE**-Kelly (couverture e p. 27) ; **IMG**-Monika (p. 13), Lydie (p. 124b) ; **PARALLÈLE**-Stéphanie Chrayen (p. 43).

BEAUTY FOOD by **marie claire**

Editorial Director: Thierry Lamarre.
Concept, interviews and Editing: Josette Milgram.
Layout editing: Nicolas Valoteau.
Assistant editor: Either Studio.
Editorial assistant: Adeline Lobut.
Artwork and design: Domitille Peyron and Sylvie Creusy, assisted by Audrey Lacoudre.
Translation: Kim Allen Gleed

First published in French by
Editons MARIE CLAIRE in 2007(c) 2007,
Editions Marie Claire – Société d'Information
et de Créations (SIC)

This edition
published in 2010 by Murdoch Books Pty Limited

Murdoch Books Australia
Pier 8/9
23 Hickson Road
Millers Point NSW 2000
Phone: +61 (0) 2 8220 2000
Fax: +61 (0) 2 8220 2558
www.murdochbooks.com.au

Murdoch Books UK Limited
Erico House, 6th Floor
93–99 Upper Richmond Road
Putney, London SW15 2TG
Phone: +44 (0) 20 8785 5995
Fax: +44 (0) 20 8785 5985
www.murdochbooks.co.uk

The National Library of Australia Cataloguing-in-Publication Data:

Milgram, Josette.
marie claire Beauty Food / Josette Milgram
ISBN 9781741966190 (pbk.)
marie claire fashion and beauty series
Includes index.
Beauty, personal. Nutrition. Food
613.2

PRINTED IN CHINA